CHALLENGES TO INDIAN COMMERCE AND BUSINESS

CHALLENGES TO INDIAN COMMERCE AND BUSINESS

Edited by

P.N. SINGH

Professor and Head,
University Deptt. of Economics

and

Director
Academic Staff College (U.G.C. Sponsored)
B.R.A. Bihar University,
Muzaffarpur

DEEP & DEEP PUBLICATIONS

F-159, Rajouri Garden, New Delhi-110027

Contents

Preface

I express my deep sense of gratitude to the Executive Committee of the Indian Commerce Association for assigning me this onerous but noble task of bringing out a volume of the lectures delivered in the sacred memory of the distinguished teachers of Commerce and Management of whom some of them were the past presidents of the Indian Commerce Association. The Indian Commerce Association deserves all appreciations for initiating of late a healthy tradition of organising lectures on the eve of its annual conferences to perpetuate the memory of noted scholars and teachers in the field of Commerce and Management who have made valuable contributions not only to the growth of the subject but have also strengthened this national organisation of the teachers of Economics, Commerce and Management.

It was really a tough task to search out the memorial lectures delivered in All India Commerce Conference from the different issues of the *Indian Journal of Commerce.* I would like to put on record the help and assistance that I received in this regard from Dr. B. Narayan, Past President of the Indian Commerce Association; Dr. B.P. Singh, Executive Vice-President of the Indian Commerce Association; Dr. Ram Sagar Singh, Professor of Commerce, B.R.A. Bihar University, Muzaffarpur and Dr. A.K. Singh of Department of Commerce, Satyawati College, Delhi.

The memorial lectures delivered in or before the 50th Annual Conference of the Indian Commerce

Association held at Hyderabad in 1996 have been included in this volume. The themes that have been touched by the learned authors include—Excellence in Business Education, Environment: Past Experiences and Future Challenges, Dimensions of Marketing in 2000 A.D., Sustainable Human Development: Dimensions, Challenges and Policy-Orientations, The Interest Rate Muddle, Economic Liberalisation, Development and Quality of Human Life, Foreign Investment and India's Fragile Economy, Industrial Finance and Banking in India and Economic Commercialisation.

I experienced some difficulties again while contemplating to give an appropriate title to the book under reference, which can take care of the contents of all the papers included in this volume. Titling the book as "Challenges to Indian Commerce and Business" was the product of that thought process. I borrowed a part of the title from one of the papers of Prof. Om Prakash which has found a place in this book. All the papers, somehow or other have highlighted some issues and hinted at emerging challenges being thrown before the economy in the areas like business education, environment, marketing, human development, interest rate, economic liberalisation, foreign investment, industrial finance and banking, etc.

The lecture 'Excellence in Business Education' which figures at first place in this book was delivered by Prof. G.C. Agrawal in the memory of Dr. A. Das Gupta in XLV All India Commerce Conference held at Bangalore. Prof. Agrawal feels an urgent need for bringing out suitable changes in the outdated and irrelevant course-contents of business education in India. This would mean that the commerce education must alter its concept, contents and construction. It must aim at developing talents to the point of excellence in any of the area that job market demands. Commerce, management and vocationalised training should be treated as the parts of a single corpus of social efforts. The future of business-education lies in making it more rational and relevant. He concludes that commerce education is more in the nature of pure theory, whereas management education has greater pragmatic-orientation towards methods of efficient management. These two should come closer and supplement each other. The business education should receive public sector-orientation and private sector support.

The second paper entitled 'Environment : Past Experiences and Future Challenges' by Dr. B.P. Singh is Prof. V.K.R.V. Rao Memorial Lecture, which was delivered by Dr. Singh in XLVI All India Commerce Conference. Dr. Singh has emphasised the growing importance of the concept of sustainable growth. He gives an account of the past experiences in this regard and identifies the challenges ahead. He looks at the international dimensions of the problem and the present state of damage done to eco-system by erratic industrialisation and unplanned urbanisation process, pursued by developed economies of the world.

Although, there are plenty of instances to evidence the international initiative to contain the environmental pollution, yet the achievements are not very encouraging. The developing countries harbour suspicions that multilateral environmental deliberations are disguised attempts to keep them economically disadvantaged.

Dr. Singh feels that there is need to develop an appropriate technology and policies for achieving the desired rate of growth without lessening the long-term production potential of soil and water. Such strategy must stress on economic efficiency, political acceptability, legal framework and its enforcement, administrative feasibility and development of institutions to manage the whole system.

The third paper included in this volume is 'Dimensions of Marketing in 2000 A.D.' written by Dr. B. Narayan for Q.H. Farooqui Memorial Lecture. This lecture was delivered by him in the honour of the great professor at XLVIII Conference of the Indian Commerce Association held at Kakatiya University, Warangal.

In this paper Dr. Narayan states that the marketing activities, concepts and strategies are bound to change due to changing situations and environment. In the present liberalised situation the Indian market is exposed to several challenges. The survival of Indian companies and brand depends not only on brand but on product and the people who run the company. There is lack of commitment to product quality in the Indian producers. Another important challenge is from the technology side, because people look for a product that has a good image and is backed by good technology. Thus the changing economic scenario will force the domestic producers to adopt a new production strategy and a new marketing technique.

Dr. Narayan finds that in the world market, India has great potential in service sector and agricultural sector after liberalisation of the economy. There is yet another market in ready-made garments. The issues in marketing are to understand the consumer needs and anticipate their expectations. There is also the need to understand the consumer behaviour and change the approach of strategic marketing.

The fourth paper which finds a place in this book is 'Sustainable Human Development: Dimensions, Challenges and Policy Orientations' by Prof. B.P. Singh of Delhi School of Economics. This paper was presented by Prof. Singh in the memory of Prof. S.C. Tandon, Professor and Dean of the Faculty of Commerce and Business, Delhi School of Economics in the 48th Annual Conference of the Indian Commerce Association held at Warangal.

In this learned paper Dr. Singh attempts at providing a conceptual framework to sustainable human development. He briefly examines its dimensions, identifies challenges and sets the direction of policy orientation. The real foundation of human development is universalism in acknowledging the life claims of every one. Development must enable all individuals to enlarge their human capabilities and provide opportunities to their fullest possible use. The human development approach favours the central role of human capital in enhancing human productivity. Sustainable human development implies that current consumption cannot be financed for long by incurring economic debts that others must repay. It entails that resources must be used in ways that do not create ecological debts. It also implies sufficient investment in education and health.

Dr. Singh concludes that human development should be seen as a major contribution to sustainability. Sustainability requires far reaching changes in both national and global policy orientations. Sustainable human development strategies must ensure a sustainable livelihood for all. These strategies must have sufficient focus on poverty reduction, employment generation and social integration at the national level.

The paper titled, "The Interest Rate Muddle" figures at the fifth place in this book. This is the full text of the lecture delivered by Prof. Om Prakash in the honour of late Prof. M.K. Ghosh and late Prof. S.P. Vijaya Saradhi in the 48th All India Commerce Conference hosted by Kakatiya University, Warangal (A.P.) on January 31st 1987. In this thought-provoking paper Prof. Om Prakash tries to analyse the trend of interest rates in a critical manner and comes to the conclusion that interest rates in India have presented a muddled state of affairs. The irony is that there is enough credit within the economy, but it is quite expensive. Another contradiction has been the existence of concessional interest rates for agriculture and priority sector but the proportion of such credit has been very low. Strangely enough, the commercial banks find executes of their non-profitability in this. The interest rate policy of the Government of India has also failed to control inflation in recent years. The frequent changes in the interest rates have further complicated the issue.

Prof. Om Pakash concludes that the persistent disparity between nominal and real interest rates call for a reduction in price inflation rate of zero, so that genuine investors may have a fair deal, frequent changes in interest rates be discouraged, the gap between the commercial lending rate and the maximum interest rate available on term deposits need to be narrowed down, the tax on interest rate should be abolished and the academicians should be consulted while deciding the interest policy.

Dr. P.N. Singh's paper, 'Economic Liberalisation, Development and Quality of Human Life' which has been put on the sixth position in the contents of the book is the text of Prof. C.D. Singh Memorial Lecture which was delivered by Dr. Singh in the XLIX All Indian Commerce Conference held at Jaipur. In this paper Dr. Singh has made an attempt to visualise the impact of the development on the quality of human life in liberalised economic system which has invaded today all other systems.

Dr. Singh asserts that the key to effective economic development are equity, participation, self-reliance, sustainability and holistic approach to community life. A development strategy that can led to improvement in the quality of human life hinges on a concept of sustainable human development which entails poverty reduction, employment generation and social integration. What is needed is people-oriented development model, which can maximise social production. The present economic regime of liberalisation and globalisation has led to slashing down the expenditure on mass education and general health care thus retarding the growth of human capital. A people-oriented economic development programme must benefit the poor peasant, small and marginal farmers and workers. It must ensure right to work and decent living. Search for a just and sustainable system of production and distribution has never been so urgent as now.

Dr. Singh sums up that the cost of globalisation even when India is far from integrating with the global economy with its limited status as a trading nations have begun to bite. It has become evident that the major industrial nations play the rules of the game. The pace of reforms in India has been very slow. It has failed to achieve even the short term goal of restoring fiscal stability. An important factor determining the quality of life of India's people is the quality of public goods and services provided by all levels of government. The jobless higher growth that we have achieved is no growth. The liberalisation process should not lose the sight of the human face. The economic growth need not subordinate social development. Capitalism has now entered into a critical phase. The present economic scene is dominated by three major structural transformation-end of eurocentricity, emergence of globe as single operational unit and change in the pattern of human relationship. A system that places growth above all other goals increases social and environmental costs, generates jobless growth and derogates the rights of workers.

The noble task of delivering memorial lectures was assigned to Prof. Om Prakash, second time at Hyderabad Conference. He delivered Sir Padampat Singhania Memorial lecture in this 50th Annual Conference of the Indian Commerce Association. 'Foreign Investment and India's Fragile Economy' was the theme. This paper has been placed at the serial No. seventh in the contents of the present volume.

Prof. Om Prakash gives an idea about the foreign investment scenario in India, during the post-liberalisation period. It has been observed that only half of the total approved foreign collaboration between the first of August, 1991 and the 31st of July, 1996 could be deemed to be really relevant for India's basic growth. TELCOM is the only sector which has manifested some quick movement of a core character. Indian economy has been fragile all along during these five years of economic liberalisation

(1991-96). Inability to control fiscal deficits has fractured the Indian economy. Another matter of serious concern for India's domestic economy is the neglect of agriculture and the rural sector.

The learned professor in this thought-provoking and inspiring address suggests that a completely open door policy regarding foreign investment is self-defeating and it should be confined to core technology. Secondly, greater reliance should be placed on domestic savings. Thirdly, instead of maximising revenue collection, the government should concentrate on minimising expenditure. Fourthly, while approving foreign investment proposal, the likely liability in respect of outflow on account of interest, dividend, repatrialism, etc. should be weighed in balance. Lastly, move to privatise established financial institutions like L.I.C., G.I.C. which have stood the test of time should be discouraged. Nationalised banks should neither be merged nor privatised.

The eighth paper of the volume is 'Industrial Finance and Banking in India: A Changing Profile'. This paper was prepared by Dr. D.S. Ganguly for Prof. S.K. Basu Memorial Lecture which was delivered by him at XLII All India Commerce Conference held at BIT Mesra, Ranchi (Bihar). This paper has its focus on structural changes visible in industrial finance and banking in seventies. Significant change in the commercial banking sector was visualised after 1970 following nationalisation of banks. The bank credit expanded. The development banks established themselves as the pillars of strength in the process of reshaping the economy of the country. The composition of money market as well as capital market underwent sea change. The capital market in India was forging ahead towards maturity. Innovations in the form of instruments both in the money market and capital market were notable features. There had been massive fund flow from external financial institutions like IBRD, IMF, IDA, etc. to underdeveloped economies.

Prof. Ganguly underlines the two important facets of Indian monetary system—firstly, irrationality of money supply and regulatory approach to interest rate, and secondly, fueling inflation beyond tolerable limits. He suggests that financial discipline will have to be enforced in order to make the monetary system behave in compatibility with the dynamism of Indian economy. The notion of inter-bank competitiveness is erroneous in as much as the whole gamut of banking is under control of a central authority where the banks are less free to move beyond a limit. Indian banks have to be restructured on a functional approach and regionalised sectoral banking activity.

The last paper titled 'Economic Commercialisation' written by Prof. T.P. Maitin is the text of the R.P. Raj Bahak Memorial Lecture which was delivered at XLVII All India Commerce Conference. With the help of this paper Prof. Maitin makes an attempt to examine some issues relating to economic commercialisation. This policy of privatisation or commercialisation is now being extended to administration. Quite a good number of essential activities which were considered to be exclusive area of state responsibility for long are being handed over to private management. This trend reflects the failure of the State machinery in providing an effective management of basic affairs. The move towards excessive commercialisation ultimately makes people suffer. Such move should be checked. Management of essential activities need to be more cost effective. Shifting of such responsibilities to the private operators does not serve the purpose in a realistic manner.

A brief profile of the Past Presidents of Indian Commerce Association and distinguished scholars in whose memory the lectures which form the contents of this volume were delivered in the Annual Conferences of the Indian Commerce Association, is as follows:

I. PROF. A. DAS GUPTA

Late Prof. A. Das Gupta is considered as the father of Management education in India. He enriched the field of Commerce, Management and Business Education in his own humble ways. Virtually he played a leadership role in these fields for more than a decade. He had a long association with several companies and business houses of the country as director and policy makers. His pupils are spread all over the country as teachers and practising managers. He always aspired for enhancing the status of Commerce and Management education in the country. He worked for it and lived for it. He was Professor, Head and Dean of Faculty of Management Studies of Delhi University, Delhi. He had authored several books, which serve as pace-setters in the field of Management. He delivered his address as the President of the Indian Commerce Association at Hubli in 1958.

II. PROF. V.K.R.V. RAO

Prof. Rao, the former President of the Indian Commerce Association, who delivered his presidential address in the Sixth Annual Conference of the association held in 1952 in Delhi University, Delhi, was a legendry figure in ways more than one. He was a distinguished economist, an effective administrator, a good planner and a seasoned statesman. For some times, he was the Minister of Education in the Central Cabinet. He was a true socialist and a nationalist to the core of his heart. He had a long association with Delhi School of Economics, Delhi University, Delhi. His main contribution that deserves special mention is Deficit Financing, Capital formation and Price Behaviour in an underdeveloped economy.

His first book titled "Taxation of Income in India" was published in 1931 when he was 23 years old. He was the student of Cambridge and did his Ph.D. also from there. As a student of Cambridge he came in touch with great teachers of economics like Keynes, Pigou and Joan Robinson. Prof. Rao was one of the founders of Delhi School of Economics, Delhi Institute of Economic Growth, Delhi and Institute for Social and Economic

Change, Bangalore. In this way he was a great institution builder also.

III. PROF. Q.H. FAROOQUI

Prof. Farooqui had been one of the pillars of Commerce education in India. He had a long association with the activities of the Indian Commerce Association. He was the founder member of the Deptt. of Commerce of Aligarh Muslim University and he retired from there as Professor and Head of the Deptt. of Commerce, Prof. Farooqui was an effective teacher, a serious researcher, and a known scholar in the field of Commerce. He has been always worried to make commerce education a professional one.

IV. PROF. B.C. TANDON

Prof. Bharat Chandra Tandon was born on the 22nd June, 1933 at Allahabad. He obtained his Master of Commerce degree in 1952 from Allahabad University and was awarded D. Litt. degree by the same University in 1974. He had a brilliant academic career.

He started his teaching career from Allahabad University after a brief stay at D.N. College, Jabalpur. He moved to Kurukshetra University as Professor and Head of Commerce in 1978. From there he left for Delhi and joined the Faculty of Management Studies, University of Delhi as professor. He rose to the position of the Dean of the Faculty of Commerce and Business.

He has authored half a dozen books and has made valuable contribution in the areas of entrepreneurship development, economic planning, business environment and research methodology. He had to his credit more than thirty research papers published in various journals. He successfully guided nearly twenty research scholars leading to the award of Ph.D. degree to them. Dr. Tandon was a great teacher, an eminent scholar and a pious soul.

V. PROF. S.P. VIJAYA SARADHI

Prof. S.P. Vijaya Saradhi is remembered with great respect and regard for laying the solid foundation of Commerce and Management Education at Warangal, Andhra Pradesh. He had the capability to combine spiritual knowledge with the more material dimensions of the discipline of Commerce and Management Science in the midst of modern paradigms and their numerous manifestations. He was a great teacher of the teachers of Commerce and his pupils are spread throughout the State maning the Commerce Departments. He was a man of missionary zeal and work was worship for him.

VI. PROF. M.K. GHOSH

Late Prof. Mohit Kumar Ghosh was the first Professor and Head of the Department of Commerce of Allahabad University. He was the founder of the Indian Commerce Association. Its first annual conference was held in 1947 at Lucknow University, Lucknow. Prof. Ghosh presided over the 2nd Annual Conference which was hosted by Calcutta University in the year 1948.

Apart from being a great scholar he was an embodiment of objectivity, fairness and transparacy in administration. He was a great organiser.

VII. PROF. C.D. SINGH

Prof. C.D. Singh, one of the past presidents of the Indian Commerce Association, was born on the 14th January, 1927. He did his graduation from Patna University, Patna and M.Com. from B.H.U. Varanasi, where he secured first class first position in the University. He received his Ph.D. Degree from Cornel (U.S.A.) in 1964.

Dr. Chandradeo Singh started his career as a teacher from H.D. Jain College, Arrah (Bihar) in 1950, served

Patna University for sometime, became Reader of Commerce in Bihar University in 1954 and Professor in Bhagalpur University in 1965. He retired as Professor, Head and Dean of Commerce, Bhagalpur University, Bhagalpur in 1989.

Dr. Singh served as the Vice-Chancellor of Magadh University, Bodh-Gaya and L.N. Mithila University, Darbhanga. The U.G.C. gave due recognition to his scholarship by appointing him National Lecturer and putting him to the Panel of Commerce and Business Administration. As a distinguished teacher he was associated with several academic bodies and selection committees of different Universities. He addressed All India Commerce Conference in Burdwan in 1988 as president of the I.C.A. He has authored nearly half a dozen books. He had to his credit supervising of four researches leading to the award of D.Litt. and twenty-nine researches leading to the award of Ph.D. degrees.

VIII. SIR PADAMPAT SINGHANIA

Sir Padampat Singhania captained the Indian Commerce Association as its first president and remained in the front row of Indian businessmen for as long as half a century. He addressed the first annual conference of the Indian Commerce Association hosted by Lucknow University, Lucknow in 1947. He was born on the 3rd February, 1905. His ancestors had migrated from Rajasthan to Kanpur. His father Lala Kamalpat Singhania was the first Indian to set up cotton mill in Kanpur. After the death of his father, he assumed managerial leadership of J.K. Group of Companies founded by his father. He died in 1979 at the age of 74.

Sir Singhania was the founder of J.K. Institute of Applied Physics, Allahabad, which was inaugurated in 1949 and dedicated to the nation by Pandit Jawaharlal Nehru in 1956. He also owes credit for establishing J.K. Institute of Sociology and Human Relations at Lucknow which flourished under the academic leadership of Dr. Radhakamal Mukherjee. He had his hand in the establishment of I.I.T., at Kanpur, an institution which he nursed as Chairman of the Board of Governors for seven years. Though he was not inducted into much of formal education, his interest in higher and technical education was abiding. He became President of the Federation of the Indian Chamber of Commerce and Industry in 1935 at the young age of 30. He was a Member of the Constituent Assembly of India and Provincial Parliament in 1950.

IX. PROF. S.K. BASU

Dr. S.K. Basu was a distinguished teacher. He delivered the presidential address to the 10th All India Commerce Conference hosted by Bihar University at Ranchi, Bihar. He has authored several books.

X. DR. R.P. RAJ BAHAK

Late Dr. Ram Prasad Raj Bahak was head of the Department and Dean, Faculty of Commerce and Business Administration of Tribhuwan University, Kathmandu, Nepal. He was a great teacher and was widely respected by his students and academicians. He has authored several books and contributed papers to national and international journals. He was a forceful speaker. For sometimes he was the State Minister for Industries in the Kingdom of Nepal. I first met him at Kathmandu when he was a minister and I was also State Minister for Finance in Bihar. It was a sheer coincidence that both of us were teachers of business economics and management and were also holding ministerial positions in our respective homeland at the same time. I was very much impressed by his scholarship and administrative skill. He was a man of vision and was always worried about the development of the economy of Nepal and removal of the state of poverty of his people.

I will be failing in my duty if I do not mention the names of my esteem colleagues in the Department—Dr. J.K. Singh, Dr. R.R. Singh, Dr. F. Hussain, Dr. P.K. Roy, Dr. B.N.P. Singh, Dr. U.S.P. Singh, Dr. D.K. Das, Dr. A.K. Sinha, Dr. K.M. Prasad, Dr. S. Sengupta and Dr. C.K.P. Shahi from whom I have always received all sorts of assistance and support.

I once again express my deep sense of gratitude to the office-bearers of the Indian Commerce Association and its members spread all over the country for the confidence posed in me while assigning this noble task of compiling the memorial lectures delivered so far and giving them the shape of a book.

How can I forget the role of two new guests—my grand daughter Rishu and grand son Devasish Anand who have joined my large family. They have done their best in keeping me in good honour and fine spirit, sitting by my side and giving entertaining childish talks and laughs in course of doing this job of editing.

In the end, I thank Deep & Deep Publications for publishing this book in time and making it available for release on the occasion of the 51th Annual Conference of the Indian Commerce Association.

Muzaffarpur P.N. SINGH

List of Contributors

G.C. Agrawal, Professor and Head, Deptt. of Commerce and Business Administration, University of Allahabad, Allahabad.

B.P. Singh, Professor, Head and Dean, Faculty of Commerce and Business, Delhi School of Economics, University of Delhi, Delhi.

B. Narayan, Advisor, Birla Institute of Scientific Research and Former Professor and Head, Deptt. of Management, B.I.T. Mesra, Ranchi.

Om Prakash, Former Vice-Chancellor, University of Rajasthan, Jaipur and First National Fellow in Commerce.

P.N. Singh, Professor and Head, Director, Academic Staff College (U.G.C. Sponsored), B.R.A. Bihar University, Muzaffarpur, Former Professor of Management, B.I.T. Mesra, Ranchi and Former State Minister of Finance, Government of Bihar, Patna.

D.S. Ganguly, Former Professor and Head, Deptt. of Commerce, Burdwan University, Burdwan, West Bengal.

T.P. Maitin, Professor and Dean, Faculty of Commerce, Patna University, Patna, Bihar.

1

*Excellence in Business Education**

G.C. AGRAWAL

I feel delighted and honoured at the invitation that Professor Samiuddin has extended to me on behalf of the Indian Commerce Association to deliver Dr. A. Das Gupta Memorial Lecture. Professor Das Gupta, the former President of Indian Commerce Association was one among few who wanted the status of education in business and management to go up. He worked for it and lived for it. It will be no exaggeration to say that he made most notable contributions to the business education in India. I have used the word "Business" because the contributions of Professor Das Gupta were unparalleled both in the field of Commerce as well as Management and in fact Commerce and Management should be taken as supplementary and not competitive areas of business. His pupils are today all over the country as teachers in the universities and as executives in business and government. I was privileged to be in closeness with Professor Das Gupta. I had met first in 1958 and then

* The present paper is the full text of the lecture delivered by Prof. Agrawal in the memory of Dr. Das Gupta.

my association with him was of diverse nature. I alongwith many of his admirers will always remember him for what he did to develop teachers of business education and for his abiding faith in the ability of Indian teachers to train potential manager. I hope that in honouring his memory we can use and build on the base that Professor A. Das Gupta had build for us and enlarge and sharpen the perspective he had set for us. With this end in view I have termed the talk of the day as "Excellence in Business Education" and will like to take this opportunity of diagnosing the problem facing us today while planning for the advancement of business education. In doing so I propose to examine the relationship between Commerce and Management and would put before this august body few ideas for closer scrutinity and action-oriented orientation.

Business Education is concerned with the study of problems of business. Problems of the operation of business units therefore deserve dispassionate and scientific study. These are studied in the various branches of Business Science like the Science of Commerce, the Science of Business Management and other trans-disciplinary business sciences including Vocational Science. Whenever we talk of Commerce we have to consider it as a part of the bigger system and having wider objective.

The Science of Commerce has to develop by itself the capacity to face the challenge of a growing society and from this point of view the problems confronting it are varied and complex. This is so because the pattern of business is changing fast. Educated persons of younger ages and cosmopolitan outlook are going to top positions. According to one survey in India about 53 per cent of the recent group of Presidents are graduates and average age of the newer presidents is between 50-52 years which is lower by 2 years than that of their counterparts a decade ago. Further the technical and specialist positions of strategic importance are being held by young and cosmopolitan persons having received the impression of the culture of technological society which reflects in their thinking and living styles who have razorsharp brains and familiarity with a whole host of new scientific and social techniques which provide vastly increased capacities to handle nature and man. In course of time they are bound to occupy Senior position. As the owner-manager loses his position and competence rather than on age or domination begins to attract responsibility, the entry of young technologists, social technicians and management graduates in managerial cadres will become more common.

I feel assured through contacts with these youngmen when I see that we have in our country young persons who are destined to take the nation forward on the road of progress. To be meaningful therefore, the Science of Commerce has to give upto itself a clear and definite objective and to develop a whole set of plans and strategies to achieve it. This is a tremendous task and needs rebuilding almost from the very foundation, undertaking a good deal of research work, re-orientation of attitudes and thinking of the faculty and the development of new teaching and investigational capacities. At the same time it has to work for achieving integration with the stream of Business Management. It has to get ready to receive and incorporate the maximum of trans-disciplinary radiation, and to have close link with quantitative and behavioural sciences. Quantitative techniques will indicate associations, correlations and group relationship while behavioural sciences will provide an insight into human motivations, group functioning and cultural rooted behaviours thereby seeking explanations for the interrelations and discovering new sources of motivating the human factor.

Business education in India has been suffering from Myopia. There is an urgent need for a thorough heart search even before the attempt to comprehend its new dimensions. This would, involve historical analysis also.

It was only towards the end of the last century that social awakening had spread the spirit of rational analysis of human engagements and interests and the business activities emerged as a subject worthy of formal education. The Wharton School of Finance and Commerce in the University of Pennsylvania in 1881 was the first Institution of its kind and in UK the university education in commerce began around 1900. In India, however, this did not begin until just before the World War I. By 1930 it came to be recognised as an independent and separate academic discipline. However, it was only in 1961 that the Special Committee for Commerce Education (Rao Committee identified) Commerce as a distinct educational stream.

The structural framework of business education in India is made up of commerce education, professional Institution—statutory and specialised and management education. The institutional formation is composed of the university faculties of commerce, the statutory professional bodies and the special institutions dealing with functional areas in specific segments of business and the institutes of management and university faculties of management.

What is Commerce? Tentatively Commerce can be explained as a science which studies business as a human activity and human behaviour in the conduct of business activities. The former consists of five broad divisions viz., industry, trade, banking, insurance and transport and commerce studies each one of these trying to identify their specific nature and needs. But Commerce also seeks to comprehend human behaviour in the conduct of each of these five divisions at the conceptual level in intellectual understanding and at the concrete level of generating operational knowledge for proficiency in the performance of these activities.

Commerce is thus a science as it seeks to discipline the faculties of human mind through the scientific methodology. But as a science it has not build up a massive base of theories and principles and has not established laws which explain behaviour. Similarly, Commerce is not a positive science since it does not deal with inert matter where the cause effect relationship is fixed and the reactions are predictable and which can be experimentally demonstrated. It deals with live consciousness of human being which can be understood only by understanding the internal consciousness of the people which are expressed in terms of intentions, attitudes and motivation. This provides commerce a different position for three reasons: (a) the impossibility of conducting experiments, (b) the lack of generalised units of measurement, and (c) the complexity of business through knowledge. It uses knowledge generated by various disciplines and also creates a new form of knowledge viz. knowledge to use knowledge by way of Order, System, Speed and Method. The knowledge component of Commerce is fast expanding and getting stronger. As the social culture shifts its focus from the ideal to material, Commerce education has started moving from abstract thinking to thoughtful action. The emphasis is moving ahead from principles of pragmatism. Perception and practices are getting prominence over theoretical explorations. The knowledge component of commerce has multidimensions including quality of a liberated mind, business as a phenomenon. Businessman and his behaviour, regulatory framework of business and institutions set of business.

OBJECTIVES AND TASKS OF COMMERCE EDUCATION

The objectives of commerce education should be identified with the objectives of university education. But in doing so the unique environmental characteristics influencing the business education have to be kept in view. Too much government due to historical-socio-economic reasons is the most important. Lack of work culture is the other. Here work is not worshipped but worship work. Steep economic and regional disparities in living standards and low standard of education are also of equal weight. But the most important is that ours is a mini world with multi-national characteristics. The Radhakrishnan Commission on University Education was not clear about the objectives of the commerce education. But Rao Committee (1961) was of the view that the primary objective of the commerce education was to impart liberal education of the same kind as in other subjects but with a business bias. The tasks of the commerce education in universities however could be of various types. It could be a transfer function aiming at acquiring and analysing knowledge generated by the various disciplines of mind and adapting knowledge and techniques for making them appropriate for the business. It could have teaching dimension aiming at providing a stimulating learning experience with a view to create capabilities and attainment of potential in the students. Finally, the Research aspect would aim at strengthening the knowledge component in areas of teaching material, changes in the society and business, meeting the changes taking place and in finding out ways and means of expending the desired changes is business activities and ethics.

CHANGING PROFILE OF COMMERCE EDUCATION

The profile of commerce education is very rapidly changing and has assumed a new picture. The outlines are shifting to make the total visual impression different. This would mean that the commerce education must alter is concept, contents and construction. And sooner it its done, this discipline will attain new direction and dimension. In this age of discontinuity and disquiet we have to be guided by the tenet of social relevance. But the test of relevance itself keeps changing. What was relevant yesterday shall not remain relevant tomorrow. Then, what is relevant for one group of the society may not be accepted as relevant by the other groups. Therefore, important questions to be answered are: How to determine what is relevant? Who should determine relevance? Whether the teacher of Commerce alone have the right to decide what to teach and how to reach? What should be the role of the students, parents and employers? However the maximisation of competitive competence in the students opting for commerce may be the true test of relevance. The critical factor in success in life is ability to compete, not alone the academic excellence. The history of human society also confirms that academic success is not directly related to success in life outside the academy. Under the existing pattern of priorities the required areas of competences are the proficiency to work with idea, work with data, to work with people and to work with things. The university commerce education must aim to develop talent to point of excellence in any of the area which the students choose to pursue. The focus of competences generated shall be preparing young people to win success at the open tests conducted by the various governments and private users of manpower. The curriculum of study shall be no more turned to the requirements of obtaining a degree. The Indian society has touched the point of momentous changes. New approaches and expectations are opening up the Indian economy and the pressure of competition is a felt presence now. The commerce educators and planners must actively monitor the social changes and remain ready to adopted new priorities and to reconstructs their structure. Out of the various priorities mention may be made about rural bias and computer revolution. The structure of the society is increasingly adjusting to rural youth, rural power and rural attitudes. This rural bias is moving the Indian society from the flower-culture to the root-culture, from the elitist to the rustic. For commerce educators this is a call for alert readiness to make expensive adaptations in their course objectives, course designs and course conduct. Then technology has been the handmade of the business since the Industrial revolution. But it was confined to the factories and production processes. With the advent of computer age, technology has engulfed business in all its aspects. It has changed not only the methodology but is changing the mind and the manner of thinking.

STRATEGY FOR COMMERCE EDUCATION

On the basis of past experience some guidelines for exploring and extending the frontiers of commerce as a discipline can be pin-pointed. There is the need for adopting systems approach in strategy formulation. In designing the strategy we have to handle the new realities and satisfy the new organisational needs of business and society. A system is sustained by its inner rationale. In commerce education the rationale so far has been the logic of gaining acceptance as a discipline of mind. There is the need for shift in this rationale. The logic of market place where quality, utility, competitiveness, selection and compromise dominate will have to be given strategic importance. Commerce education must take the responsibility of shifting from manual to mechanical, routine to contingent, slow to fast. The nature of task-skills is also shifting from single variable to multi-variable handing. The mannual manpower is to be transformed into knowledge worker manpower. As the frontiers expand our reach must expand. In the five major divisions of business activity (industry, trade, banking, insurance and transport) the forces which are expanding the frontiers are: (i) service as industry is superceding, manufacturing, and (ii) self-employment is superceding other career opening for young people. There is thus limitless opportunity for growth of commerce education by timely extension and diversification of commerce courses.

CO-ORDINATION BETWEEN THE CONSTITUENTS OF BUSINESS EDUCATION

The co-ordination between the three constituents of business education is inevitable and the need for establishing appropriate links is most urgently needed. There is the need to sell the idea that commerce, management and vocalised training are the parts of single corpus of social efforts. They are supplementary and not competitive. All the three have the common purpose i.e., preparing manpower for various positions and purposes in any business unit. The need is to generate a spirit of mutual understanding and reciprocal relationship so that all the three parts may enhance their contribution to the service of business and society. Commerce educators should not research for one best way or one final answer to the problems of the commerce education. Part of the education crisis today lies in this mistaken belief. This may lead to the negation of exploration and experimentation, idea generation and maturation, creativity and ingenuity in a field of such vital concern as Commerce.

Commerce education is the main tree which has branched off into several areas. But the main trunk has to be kept in tact. The objectives of commerce education at degree level will have to be different than the post graduate level. At the graduate level its objectives may be three-fold: (i) to make it a terminal degree so as to enable one to make up self-employment; (ii) to provide required skills to pursue higher education including professional examinations, and (iii) to make it job-oriented. At the post-graduate level the the objectives may be: (i) to develop functional/sectoral specialisation with analytical skills decision-making and problem-solving capacities, and (ii) to develop skills in teaching and research and to promote entrepreneurial skills.

THE FUTURE OF BUSINESS EDUCATION

The future of business education lies in making it more rational and relevant. The overall objectives will have to be defined in clear terms and a time bound plan should be evolved. Clear demarcation of areas and the relative roles of commerce, management professional institutes and vocational schools should also be worked out and every attempt has to be made generate greater interaction with the industry and business. The business education should receive public sector orientation—

participation and care should be taken to create work culture values where productivity and excellence are the ultimate objectives. All this has to be done keeping in view the ultimate objective of integrating commerce and management education. Commerce education is more in the nature of pure theory and relates to drawing abstractions front business phenomenon and procedures and developing new trans-disciplinary business science, whereas management education has greater pragmatic orientation towards methods of efficient management. One has greater inner self-sufficiency the other is more derivative. But both have the basic unity in that their subject matter is the same. Therefore, one has to keep an open mind about their mutual relationship in future.

In conclusion, I should like to make an humble appeal to the planners in the Union Government and the various state governments, the industry and business and the educational institutions including professional institutes to work with a spirit of cooperation for the developing of commerce education which has a bright and challenging future ahead.

2

*Environment: Past Experiences and Future Challenges**

B.P. SINGH**

I must place on record my deep sense of gratitude and delight having been invited by the Indian Commerce Association to deliver Professor V.K.R.V. Rao Memorial Lecture. Professor Rao, the former President of Indian Commerce Association was a legendary figure in ways more than one. A brilliant scholar, an internationally reputed distinguished economist, an effective administrator, a pragmatic planer, an astute thinker, institution builder, a politically involved person, and a humanist to the core. Hailing from a semi-rural background and a humble economic status, Professor V.K.R.V. Rao left an indelible mark of his unique personality first as a student, then as a teacher, administrator, planner and finally as a Minister for Education in the Central Cabinet.

---

* The present paper is the full text of the lecture delivered by Dr. Singh in the memory of Prof. V.K.R.V. Rao.

** Department of Commerce, Delhi School of Economics, University of Delhi, Delhi.

India's economic development and amelioration of the lot of poor and down-trodden were the passions which inspired Professor Rao, throughout his life, and got reflected in his writings, speeches, deliberations, and approaches. He was true socialist and a nationalist to the core. As a befitting tribute to the memory of such a Great Son of India, I have chosen to shave some of my thoughts on the subject of *Environment: Past Experience and Future Challenges* dilating both on global scenario and Indian context.

The concept of growth at all costs, which governed development policies around the world until the eighties is being replaced with the idea of sustainable development in the nineties. This is the consequence of growing evidence of heavy price we have to pay for unsustainable consumption pattern, particularly of the richer countries. In the name of growth, fossil fuels have been burnt, abundant chemicals harmful to the atmosphere have proliferated, poisons have been dumped on land and in rivers and oceans, and natural resources, such as, forests have been ravaged and exploited to the point of extinction. As a result, we are confronted with the phenomenon of global warming, caused by accumulation of gases, such as, carbondioxide, and the depletion of ozonelayer.

Thus, it is clear that the concept of economic growth and environmental protection are inextricably lined, and that the quality of present and future life rests on meeting basic human needs without destroying the environment on which all life depends. This fact has been stressed by the Business Council for Sustainable Development (BSCD) which is a high level consortium of leading industrial organization. According to the declaration of this organizations "Business will play a vital role in the future health of this planet. As business leaders, we are committed to the concept of sustainable development, improving the needs of the present without compromising the welfare of the future generations."

Thus, the sustainable development implies a future in which life is improved world wide through economic development, where local environment and the bio-spheres are protected and science is mobilised to create new opportunities for human progress.

The growing importance of this concept of sustainable growth can be seen from the consequences of the development and industrial practices that are being followed by the developed and developing nations during the last few decades.

If we look at the international dimensions of the problem, we can observe that a huge quantity of harmful substances (pollutants) have been moving across national frontiers through river system and oceans. Environmental hazards originating in one country are being carried into the other neighbouring countries and beyond. Some of these have assumed global proportions like the phenomenon of "Acid rain", caused by the oxides of sulphur arising mainly from the thermal plants and automobile exhausts. The chemical process in which it affects the environment is that, the ordinary rain water after interaction with the sulphur oxide and carbon monoxide, exhausted to the air through smoke, make the water acidic, consequently when falls on the soil damages the trees, vegetation and marine life. There has been a large scale destruction of forest (in Central Europe) as a result of this precipitation through rain and snow. It has also caused damage to several historical buildings like the famous colossus of Rome and Taj Mahal of Agra (deposition of carbon dioxide and sulphur dioxide). Canada has been adversely affected by sulphur emission from power plants and exhausts. The marine life in the lakes of Norway and Sweden are damaged due to the acid rain from the industrial plants. The recent gulf war which over-shadowed the atmosphere of the eastern Europe has destroyed many species of vegetation in the Himalayan Plateau. The new concept of "Black Ice" which contained carbon monoxide and uranium effluents from the atomic explosion, has caused many genetic diseases among people using the river water flowing from the Himalayas. Another way in which the carbon dioxide contents of the smoke which arise from burning fossil fuels, coal and oil affect the environment, by having enormous heat absorbing capacity which, in turn, contributes to the global warming up which leads to melting of polar ice caps, rising water level in the oceans and inundating large coastal areas and island countries. A gradual rise of the sea level attributable to this phenomenon has been lately noticed in Bangladesh and Maldives.

Besides this, another pollutant called clorofluro carbons (CFCS) which results chiefly from aerosol sprays, refrigeration, xeroxing and air craft exhausts CFCS are believed to the thinning the ozone layer of the atmosphere* which leads to increased incidence of skin cancer and damage to animal and plant life.

As regards tarns-boundary water pollution, which follows chiefly from the fact that there are over 200 rivers or lakes which flow through two or more countries. Some of them like Amazan and Danube, Mecong, Nile etc. are shared by six or more countries. These rivers commonly carry sewage, industrial effluents, chemical residues and agricultural run-offs including chemical fertilizers and pesticides. Eventually the rivers deposit these pollutants into the oceans which affect a large number of coastal and hinterland countrics.

Another serious, international or global pollutants is the fall out from the nuclear plants like Chernobyle leak accidents. According to a noted British biologist Arther Burne, an increasing number of people are likely to die from Lukemia and other forms of cancer if nuclear tests and accidents continue unabated.

---

* Ozone layer of the atmosphere work as a protective umbrella for the earth because if stops the ultra-violet rays that emanate from the sun. The ultra-violent rays are highly harmful to the biological system as it destroys the living cells of any living body.

Furthermore, the earths fertility and recuperative powers are damaged in the long-run by deforestation, frequent use of chemical fertilizers, and by deep mechanical plough in which over exposes the more fertile top soil. The increased demand for farm land (to raise cash crops) and lucrative exports of forest products to the industrialised countries, is causing deforestation of 11 million hectare of land in the third world each year. This leads to the improvement and erosion of soil, flooding and silting of the rivers and reservoirs, as happened in Bangladesh, Nigeria and Panama and some other areas. Ultimately, it adversely affects the world food supply by cutting into the availability of arable land for food production. At the same time, thanks to the rising demographic curve, and wasteful food habits of the modern elites, the demand for food is growing. In this scenario of increasing demand for and decreasing supply of food near-famine conditions occur over large areas of the world. About 20 countries in the sub-Saharan Africa have been experiencing chronic famine condition due to this demand-supply mismatch syndrome.

Along with food, the mineral resources are also getting fast depleted due to the reckless mass production and uncontrolled consumption culture. According to a study conducted by the American National Academy of science, the major mineral resources of the world like iron-ore and tongsten, may not last for more than a hundred years at the present level of consumption, and coal and oil may exhaust even sooner.

PRESENT STATE OF DAMAGE OF ECO-SYSTEM

Apart from the above mentioned calamities what shocks more to the environmental scientists, is the present state of damage to the eco-system caused due to environmental pollution.

According to the report of the World Wafen Institute U.S.A. a minimum of 140 plants and animal species are condemned to extinction each day due to acid rains, soil erosion and industrial effluences. Forests are vanishing at the rate of 17 million hectares every year. The atmospheric level of the heat taping carbon dioxide are now 26% higher than the pre-industrial concentration. The protective ozone shield is thinning twice as fast as the scientists estimated 10 years back. Due to this, mirriads of genetic diseases are creeping into the biological system.

Besides this, the earth crust is getting warmer day by day which is adversely affecting the human and animal life.

In India, at present, nearly 70% of the available water is polluted. Over 73 million work day are lost annually due to water related diseases. Every second, about half a hectare of forest is consumed for wood; out of the total of 40 million hectares of land in India, only one quarter is irrigated. On an average, every hectare loss 20 tonnes of topsoil a year. Almost for million hectares have been swallowed up by ravines. In the last two decades in Delhi alone there has been 10-fold increase in the number of mobiles pumping pollutants into the air. It won't be a wonder, when a breath of fresh air will become a rare community in the city.

PRESENT DAY MOVEMENT TO RESERVE ECO-SYSTEM

Global

There is a historical evidence that in pre-modern times, there was awareness of the unfavourable dimensions of environmental pollution. But, following an unprecedented material boom generated by the industrial revolution, the concern for environmental and ecological problems tended to recede into the background—so much so that the League of Nations was virtually unconcerned about these issues. And, they did not figure as major problems in the early programmes of the U.N.

It was the UN conference on human environment, held in Stockholm (5-10th June, 1972) that proclaimed the environmental issues as a matter of over-whelming global concern. As a first step to deal with this vast problem, it set up the U.N. Environmental Programme (UNEP). It was the Brundtland Commission, with its emphasis that environment and development are antagonistic, but two different facets of the same issue, that gave a momentum to environment consciousness. Then came the Montreal Protocol 1987, amended under pressure from India and other developing countries in London in 1990. The damaging and alarming scientific evidence which has been pouring in, prompted the industrial countries and biggest CFC consumers who were reluctant to sign to amended protocol voluntarily.

In the global context, the scientific evidence surely indicates that it is the western industrialised nations that have contributed to the global problem e.g. annual per capita carbon emission to atmosphere in USA is 5 tonnes while that in India is 4 tonnes.

A point that is now forcefully being made by the inter-Governmental Panel on climate change (an International body of over 300 scientists drawn from 100 countries) is that 25% of the world's population has contributed to 75% of the global environment problem. The growing pressure form the international community to bring about a balance in the distribution of the benefits of indutrialisation and harms of pollution between the rich and poor countries, helped the world community to go for the earth summit in Rio-de-Jenairo on 6th June, 1992, under the patronage of UNEP. The summit was a great success in terms of participation, but was a complete failure in terms of achievement of its objective. The summit estimated the total cost $ 625 billion as the cost of world environment programmes. Out of which the developed nations are paying only a meagre $ 19 billion. Since the contribution of developed nations to the world environment pollution is approximately 80%, it was argued that the developed nations should bear at least $ 125 billion and the rest $ 500 billion to be born by the developing nations. The response to this question has been negative.

India

India, as the leader of the developing countries, has shown much more concern towards environmental problems as compared to any other country of the group. The Bureau of Indian Standards (BIS) which is a central body for fixing up standards for industrial products and services, has taken into consideration the international standards for controlling pollution in India. So far the Bureau has supplied 250 standards covering codes of practice, methods of testing and specification of control equipments etc. In this respect, the bureau has prescribed modification in the production quality of petroleum products. Use of DDT, which are bio-degrading and provided procedures for recycling the paper, plastic, oil and power.

In the field of legislation also three laws have been enacted, i.e., (1) The Water (Prevention and Control of Pollution) Act, 1974, (2) The Air Prevention and Control of Pollution) Act, 1981, and (3) Environmental Protection Act, 1986. To implement these legislations the Central Pollution Board has been instituted in case of specific categories of industries. Besides this, various programmes on pollution are being aided by financial institution, municipal corporations, statutory bodies, associations of manufacturers and Government. The Ministry of Environment has also promulgated the issue of "Eco-Mark" to industrial friendly nature of the product, so that production can go on without affecting the environment. The ministry has also proposed a system of environment Audit, which is a systematic device for documenting periodic and objective evaluation of the performance of available environmental facilities, management system and equipment in the industry. After assessing the harmful effects of the accidents in hazardous industries, e.g. The Sri Ram Food and Fertilizers case and Bhopal gas disaster an important enactment, i.e. Public Liabilities Insurance Act has been passed on 1st April 1991 to compel the hazardous industries to take a public liability insurance to provide immediate financial and remedial relief to the victims of the accidents. The judiciary has also stressed the setting up of environmental courts for speedy trial of environmental cases. Besides this, a proposal for tax concession to industries adopting environmental safety in the production process is on the cards.

Despite the fact that, there has been so much of initiatives found in Government legislation, Judicial pronunciation and tax consultancy, we have been able to touch only the fringe of the problem. In the area of environmental laws one sees most clearly the weaknesses of a top-down approach. Despite plethora of environmental laws covering all aspects, from air and water pollution to waste disposal to forests and even the noise level in our cities, few offenders have been brought to books. Even when the provisions of law have been put to use, it has been because of the initiative of the public spirited individuals who have moved the courts to direct the Government to implement its own laws rather than the vigilance in the part of the implementing agency like the Central Pollution Control Board. Lack of institutions at the grass root level has also been a weakness of the implementing system in India. Another weakness is the weakest link in our regulatory machinery and administrative arrangements for monitoring and enforcing environmental standards.

CONCLUSION AND RECOMMENDATIONS

Although there are plenty of instances to evidence the international initiatives to contain the environmental pollution, yet the achievements are very few. The UN conference at Stockholm (1972), Montreal Protocol (1987) and the earth summit held in Rio-de-Jenerio (1992), have all been a great success in terms of participation and creation of awareness among the members of the world community, but have failed in bringing about a consensus on the issue of sharing the global environmental costs, i.e. investment in global environmental programmes carried on by various UN agencies for removing the environmental pollution. This is particularly because of the fact that the present global environmental politics has been characterised more by feet-dragging and denial of problems than by co-operation. Few rich countries have acknowledged that they have caused the preponderance of environmental damage and, therefore, have a responsibility to underwrite most of the transition to global sustainability. The U.S. has stonewalled even modest efforts, such as setting targets to reduce carbon emission as part of on-going negotiations to protect the global climate.

The developing countries, on the other hand, harbour suspicions that multilateral environmental deliberations are disguised attempts to keep them economically disadvantaged.

Applying old politics to new realities is a losing proposition for all, just as a new set of relationship is taking shape between the east and the west, one that dismantles mutual threats and creates a climate of economic co-operation. So is there a need for a new partnership between the wealthier countries (The "North") and the developing world (The "South")—one that embrasses the common goals of restoring the planet earth and promoting sustainable progress.

In the industrialised countries, the major concern is the maintenance of the *status-quo* in yield, because this will be more than adequate to meet their home and export needs. India, China and many other developing countries, in contrast, the challenge is how to produce more from diminishing land and water resources.

Therefore, we will have to develop appropriate technology and public policies for achieving the desired rate of growth without lessening the long-term production potential of soil and water.

Hence, the strategy to be adopted in formulation of an environmental policy should stress on:

(a) the comparatibility of our environmental policies with the existing administrative, political and legal framework,

(b) economic conditions in the country, tax structure, and complicity of instruments,

(c) political acceptability and economic efficiency.

(d) case of monitoring and enforcement, and

(e) the development of institutions to manage the whole system which has been unsatisfactory in the past in developing countries, mainly due to inadequate public participation and involvement.

3

*Dimensions of Marketing in 2000 A.D.**

B. Narayan**

I am really indebted to the president of Indian Commerce Association, Executive Vice-President, Secretary and members of the Indian Commerce Association who have given me the opportunity to deliver Q.H. Farooqui Memorial Lecture before this august body at its XLVIII conference being held at Kakatiya University, Warangal.

Prof. Farooqui had been one of the pillars of Commerce Education in India. My association with him began in 1954 December in the then All India Commerce Conference held at Jaipur. Since then as a member of Ph.D. thesis adjudicators boards of some universities and in conference and Seminars I met him several times. Dr. Farooqui and academician of par excellence has been always worried to make commerce education a

* The present paper is the full text of the lecture delivered by Dr. Narayan in the memory of Prof. Q.H. Farooqui.

** Advisor, Birla Institute of Scientific Research and Visiting Professor, Deptt. of Management, Birla Institute of Technology, Mesra.

professional education and wanted to introduce the courses which can cover the changing dimensions of Indian economy and Indian Industry so that students coming out from educational portals can suit to the dynamics of business. He was a believer of "Theory without practice is sterile, practice without theory is blind." It would be befitting to his ideology of academics that we talk about changing dimensions of Indian marketing and "Challenges and opportunities of Marketing in 2000 A.D."

The marketing activities, concepts and strategies are bound to change due to changing situations and environment. Since 1985 a competitive, customer driven economy has been emerging in India. The abolition of licensing and liberalisation of market entry regulations since July 1991 has further added impetus to this process. It has been given the final shape by the formation of WTO at Markesh. Most of the people and the industrialists have felt that whether a company wants to go for global competition or not, in the present liberalised situation the Global Competition will arrive at their door step.[1] By endorsing the final Act of the Uruguay Round the developed world has in effect endorsed free trade in a multilateral setting, a phenomenon that will work to the advantage of developing countries that need new markets.[2] Countries like India will get an opportunity through W.T.O. to negotiate better deal for itself. This can be possible only when the quality and standard of the products is improved. The policy of liberalisation has created a situation in which companies like Uniliver, Glaxo, Pepsi, Whirlpool, Philips have increased their stake of equity. New products, new brands and new formulations are being announced virtually every week, mergers and acquisitions like Brooke-Bond, Lipton designed to build competitive fortress have become more common. "Down seizing", restructuring and engineering are the words that have potent force for emboldened executives. Thus the whole market environments has undergone a severe change. India has become one of the largest emerging markets attracting substantial flows of equality investment and also consumer goods.[3] It focuses that there are challenges of improved products of advanced nations on the one hand and on the other hand if the executives have vision, foresight and creativity there can be enough opportunity for domestic products both in India and in other emerging markets.

CHALLENGES

The first challenge by opening up the Indian market is of survival of Indian companies and Indian brands. Brand here I understand should be considered as a brand crated for the Indian market and owned by a company of Indian origin. Brand building is directly related to the scale of business. Indian Companies like Lakme or Nirma do not have financial boost or technology like Hindustan Lever or Colgate Palmolive.[4] It has been the experience in the past that whichever country has permitted multinational companies to enter their market, their local brands have been wiped away. Indian brands cannot have a different situation. Though Swaminathan, S. Anklesaria Aiyar, editor of the *Economic Times* feels "A very large number of low end consumers have never heard of foreign brands and are not hungering for them". The magic of the foreign brands can not be denied. A section of new middle class identifying runs after them. If the foreign brands in the long-run become Indian or perceived as Indian like Lux, Surf, then the matter is different but a Coke will always remain foreign. What attracts the consumer towards the foreign brands produced by multinational companies (MNCs) is firstly the quality and secondly the status symbol and a new way of life.

The survival of the Indian brands will depend not only on brand, but on product, the company backing it, and the people who run that company. Each of these factors determines the state and future of the brand. For example, Amul has been promoted so consistently that no MNC will easily shake its grip on Rs. 16 crores butter market. However, majority of Indian companies do not invest consistently and also adequate amount, they want quick harvest. Those Indian brands will survive which have a very clear positioning. Brands which depend not only on the advertising buck but on the entire gamut of brand building activities and what the consumer perceives as the value delivery. The technology difference won't be as important as the speed of action, the right package at the right price, the right upgradation at the right time.[5] The products in which aesthetic function is more valuable than the physical attributes will face severe problem of survival. One may recall that recently American Consumers Forum has protested on the import of Indian Shiffon Skirts and the USA Government has issued notification to stop their imports.[6]

Another important issue related to survival of Indian brands is that there is lack of commitment to product quality in the Indian Producers. What is important is that the product should meet the consumer need. You may recall that when American Cars were best those who could afford bought them. To day when Japanese cars are the best every one wants to buy them. This is the function of quality not of origin or of brand alone. Indian brands have been isolated for 40-50 years; therefore the product quality does not stack up to international standards. In fact, branding is a process for adding distinctiveness to products or service which offer the consumer quality, value and satisfaction. Apart from Superior Quality what foreignness also signals is status and a new way of life. The producers will have to take care of this need.[7] If they do not looked after their consumers need some body else will take care for their need. By 2000 A.D. if the Indian producers do not realise these facts, they will face serious threat of losing the market. In the liberalised economy a market once won can not remain for ever for a particular company or product unless the company is continuously engaged in innovation of technology and products as per the need of the consumers.

Another important challenge is from the technology side because people look for a product that has a good image is backed by good technology. It is believed that the multinationals have better technology to back their products. Indian producers have always imported technology and have never made any attempt to Indianise them, improve upon them and have a better technology of their own. Technology imports have been costlier and will definitely increase the cost of production. To meet the challenges posed by the multinationals it is essential that the Indian producers should also use better technology. Bajaj is one example, inspite of the fact that Bajaj entered in business of two-wheelers with the imported technology, they have Indianised it and they have also continuously made effort to improve the technology and improve the product. The Bajaj scooter is one of the quality product backed by a better technology. No multinational can make Bajaj to loose it a market. If a company has invested in technology and in quality of its produce, it will survive like Bajaj and VIP Luggage because they have ensured that the product lives up to promise that they have made. Hence, the Indian producers have to upgrade, update, renovate and improve their technology to have quality product which can match the forcing products and meet the consumers need both in domestic and foreign markets. This will definitely depend upon a company's access to the technology, if it can buy the technology it is better; if not, will be compelled to enter into joint ventures or alliance with foreign companies to have access to technology. Only having the technology is not enough. There is need to invest in technology improvement and continuous up-gradation of technology. Technology and its development has become one of the essentials of economic development. We are aware that only one company of Japan invests an amount in R & D of technology which has been equal to the total amount of investment in R & D in India.

The opening of Indian market for world producers and the market of other countries for Indian producers will have any meaning only when the Indian producers have any product backed by a good technology and superior in quality to match the competitors product. Hence Indian producers need continuous innovation and investment in innovation to survive.

Everyone, who is a student of marketing might have found that in Indian market premium brands are flooding the market to block the entry of the products of MNCs. Several premium brands in the last two or three years have been priced up to 10 times higher than the popular brands.[8] This is based on the idea that as income of middle class increase and as exposure to richer classes increase, there will be demand for products which may have distinction and life style. Thus, the premium brands of Indian producers will pose a challenge to the other products. The premium brand producers are happy as they quote the survey report of National Council of Applied Economic Research that "there are 65 million middle class households earning over Rs. 18,000 per annum out of which 3.7 million earn over Rs. 78,000 per annum. One million house holds earn more than Rs. 1 lakh a year". In 1993 the purchasing power of average Indian had been equivalent to $ 1,150 (Rs. 35,650) per year. Thus, they have been guessing about the market of premium brand goods among these "Maruti Millions" or the status seekers. A host of products like Lacoste's shirt priced for Rs. 750, Park Avenue Shoes for Rs. 1600 and so on will meet the demand of the new status seeker middle class consumers. It is true that only a minuscule of Indian population will buy. These products will have a core group of buyers and large number of floating buyers. Thus the premium brand products are posing challenge to other products. Let us call it intra-country competition. The challenges will be compounded because the consumers may buy the usual brand and also the premium brands for occasional use leading to low frequency of repeat purchase of premium brands, secondly with the fast moving consumer goods consumers will float not only between brands in a product category but also between the categories themselves. Hence even the producers of premium brands will have to face problems in selling their products. Lastly, the introduction of intellectual copy right will be introduced by 2000, hence the imitation of product will be beaten down and out. The premium product producers will have to adjust to the socio-economic conditions of the country and produce products for higher price which will give value to consumers for the money paid.[9]

Thus the changing economic scenario opening up the Indian market for the global producers has definitely forced the domestic producers to adopt a new production strategy and a new marketing technique. The change definitely throws some challenges but it provides some opportunities also.

OPPORTUNITIES

Liberalisation of Indian economy and going for global and entering into an agreement to be a member of World Trade Organisations, India will now have an Institution—WTO, to negotiate better deal for itself through discussion and creating consensus among the contacting parties.[10] As Mudra's Krishnamurthy puts "the globalisation of the Indian market needs to be seen as an opportunity to become MNC, not as a problem. "Building competitive advantage through exposure to international markets should be a conscious strategy. Companies from countries like Japan and South Korea have learnt from the West and then successfully marketed world class brand globally. The Chief Executive of a Japanese car manufacturing company which was established with the help of technological assistance of General Motors after fifteen years General motors; on return he called, his executive meeting and told them that they can go for World Market now, his executives expressed doubts. They were send to visit General Motors and on return they confessed that they have improved over General Motors and can easily compete in the World Market. Now

Japanese cars are in American market and in European market competing successfully and in some cases sharing major portion of automobile market. Japan had imported Technology for Watch manufacturing from Switzerland. It is Japan which added day and dates, music and varieties of alarm sounds and finally automatic and quartz and captured major share of world watch market. Indian producers will have to learn from Japanese experience to avail the opportunity of going in foreign market. Clarity of thinking and a single mind focused strategy on improved Technology and Superior Products are key to realise the potentials and avail them. In fact, the policy of globalisation has been adopted with an idea to make Indian producer competitive globally. Hence the opportunity for Indian companies to become efficient MNCs has been provided by this situation.

Mr. Balkrishna Zutshi, Indian representative at WTO, expressed that the change in economic policy and signing of agreement with WTO provides access to global market. There is tremendous opportunity for India to integrate itself with the global market. It is now upto Indian industries and to some extent the government, to adopt the right policy to exploit the country's potential in the world market and to improve its export in different areas.

One of the new area for achieving some share in world market is the service sector. In the recent agreement some concessions have been provided for the export of services. They form a good basis for further developed. This particular area which can interest India, the movement of natural persons as service provider has tremendous opportunity. Further we can increase our exports to textiles, but we have to modernise our textile industry in next ten years. The export of textile will pick up.

India has great potential in agricultural sector. The government can subsidise upto 10% of the value of production, on fertilizer, water, pesticides, seeds and electricity. It can help in improvement of quality and quantity of product. India can export rice and other agricultural products to Japan and Korea upto 4% of their demand. Thus, the probability of export of agricultural produce has increased, exports of spices has great potential. India exported 1,50,000 tonnes of spices totalling worth Rs. 500 crores last year 1993-94.[11] Following table will show the upswing in Indian Exports

TABLE 3.1

Indian Export an Upswing

(Rs. in crore)

Year	*Value*
1990-91	53350
1991-92	69546
1992-93	53648
1993-94	72886

TABLE 3.2

Export of Agro Products

(in $ million)

Particulars	*1991-92*	*1992-93*	*1993-94*
Spices	150	127	160
Cereals	356	342	370
Oil Cakes	399	574	555
Vegetable and Processed Food	375	349	455
Sugar	165	112	176

in general and Agro-products in particular:

Cashewnuts, tobacco, cereals, processed food, sugar and tea can have greater potential for increased exports. The quality, size of packing and value addition is the need. If a group of exporters who are quality conscious, who can keep pace with international changes and bring in technology, make efforts, may open opportunity for growth of exports.

There is another area where Indian producers can think of entering into global market, the ready made garments. The Gokal Das Exports have been exporting shirts, to Europe, Australia, Middle East, Singapore, U.S.A., Canada and are regular supplier to Levi Straus and Warnglar. Even while international brand names like Pierrecardin, Benetton, Van-Heusen and Arrow are making inroads in domestic market, Indian companies are betting into high technologies to tap emerging global opportunities. Indian companies have no choice but to invest heavily in developing exclusive brands and entering into non-cotton fabrics. However, India can be a potential exporter in this area. There is enough scope of exports of shoes and other leather garments. Liberty shoes and Namaste Exports have shown the way. Korean leather garments have become costly and European markets have started opening up mainly due to the closure of tanneries there. The scope of export of leather products has increased. According to study conducted by the Federations of Indian Export Organisation "Indian exports are extremely competitive in special area like leather, garments, handloom, jewellery and engineering goods where it is much easier to adopt to changing trends of a foreigning buyer who suddenly asks for a different auto components, or a different fashion of handloom cloth or leather garments. It is much easy for a small producer to change his production process. The only need is to understand the consumer need, improve the quality of the product and add value through packaging and design. The competitive edge can be added by adopting and innovating required technology and a marketing strategy for the changing situation.

ISSUES

One can now clearly feel that the issues in marketing in 2000 A.D. are, to understand the consumer needs and anticipate their expectations whether they are in domestic market or in other countries market. In fact, in an ACME Seminar of Top executives the consensus has been that all the successful brands have designed and developed products on the basis of the anticipation of consumers' needs and expectations. The second important issue which was emphasised at the seminar by these executives was the need of being "unique", "innovative", "positioning" and therefore becoming competitive, whether they were "offering" themselves or the way they were presented and communicated to any prospective buyer. Thirdly, the executives of the companies of successful brands have confessed that the secret of the success of their company has been the product itself rather than any other marketing technique or inputs such as salesforce, advertising, promotion, quality of overall managements, etc.

If one examines, a few domestic products of wholly Indian companies one may be able to bring home the important issue of marketing for 2000 A.D., such as Nirma (Popular priced washing powder), Titan watches, ONIDA (TV) Videocon Washing machine and Maruti Cars, Maggi Noodles, and "Close Up" tooth paste each of them presents some significant break through in terms of product development.

Nirma, the most often quoted brand in almost any marketing forum in the past ten years entered with almost no backing or background in consumer marketing and in a period of five years, emerged as the greatest competitive threat ever faced by Unilever's flagship company in India, Hindustan Lever, ignored by all those in the detergent market for nearly five years as being not in our segment, not our kind of product, this brand launched at almost third of the unit price of Unilever's Surf, grew explosively almost ten-fold in a ten years period, overtook everyone else in the process. Titan a company launched by Tata, India's largest private sector entrepreneurial group repositioned the watch and especially the Indian made watch in the eye of the consumer and made it into a stylish personal accessory to both men and women.

In just four years, it grew to 2.6 million watches and No. 1 in the quartz segment and No. 2 overall behind the much older and slower, HMT, it also rewrote the 'rule book' of conventional wisdom in watch marketing, that the best watches are imported (legally or illegally).

Some of them created new segments in the market and new usages and users. You may recall ketchup, for example had long been thought of and used as an essentially western product, which could not easily be blended with Indian cuisine. Maggi by Nestle not only introduced alternatives to the tomato sauce, which has generally too blend for the discerning Indian plate, but shoed it in association with a number of essentially Indian snakes such as Samosa and Vada. An even greater innovation was the 2 minute noddle. Long known both in Europe and the Far East a meal by itself, the noddle could not be expected to replace rice or the home made forms of wheat such as pooris and chappatis. However, interestingly presented and positioned as an afternoon, after school snack, it caught the imagination of children and mother to become an almost unique product that virtually owned the territory it developed.

A few of them took competitive standards several niches higher, for example: The Maruti small car (800 cc) gave the Indian motorist a stylish, maneuverable and modern alternative with a compact design. Of course, the fact that the technology was several decades ahead of the Fiat and Morries Oxford versions (Premier Padmini and Hindustan Ambassador), ensured that it virtually had no competition. The Maruti 1000 which followed in the late 80's had an almost unique position as a "Japanese quality premium personal car. The latest offering is the Maruti Zen, the first Indian car in incorporate the jelly bean shape and round edges, to reduce wind resistance and increase fuel economy, along with five speed transmission all with the full impact of Suzuki of Japan, now the majority owner of this company. Three out of every four cars sold in India, now come from Maruti in the home appliances field little known Videocon emerged in a period 4 years as the major share leader with 27% of the colour TVs market and 50% of the washing machines market. They flooded the market with Japanese style product introduction rate, concentrating on wooing the dealers with substantially higher margins and array of incentives and beating the competition on price. In this last aspect, they had much in common with Nirma in the detergent market and Hero in bicycles and mopeds. For India's largest and most successful consumer product company, Hindustan lever, "Close Up", brought success at the last to the personal products division in the eternal battle against Colgate in the toothpaste market. Relaunched as gel with variants it attained a 15% market share. Only two of the above brands "Maggi" and "Close up" are owned and marketed by multinationals affiliates in India. All the others are not only from wholly owned Indian companies but in many cases from entrepreneurial first generation business group. Neither the Dhoots of Videoconor Mr. Patel of Nirma started with any accumulated experience in a related industry. Nor did they have the war chests from promotional onslaught which a Coke, a Pepsi or a Proctor and Gamble would subsequently bring to the Indian scene. The above examples of products and their marketing way clearly give any one to understand that being multinational *per se* cut no ICE with Indian consumers; that sheer power of resource is not a pre requisite for success and competitive edge. That what is important for being competitive in the future is to be innovative in product as per need and expectations of the consumer and therefore, there is urgency of improving the product and service quality standard; finally that innovation will have to be applied to every segment of business, retailing, general management quality, structure and even financing.

DYNAMICS APPROACH TO MARKETING

The success of the five brands mentioned above proves that there is the need to understand consumer behaviour in the Indian context and to change the approach of strategic marketing. That is succeed in any competition market whether domestic or global the application of the same approach applied prior to 91 will not be effective. What ever may be the individual ingredients of success, strategic style or approach must concentrate on rewriting the 'rule book'. In earlier decades the dictum was that marketing orientation meant not only doing things differently (the USP School) but better and more memorably (as emphasised by David Ogilvy and Ries and Trout in the brand personality and its positioning eras). To day beyond just being different or better thinking about the market and conceiving the future differently from on predecessor, seems be at the core of successful strategic marketing. The core and key factor in the above five brands has been innovation to meet the future opportunities and understanding the needs of the consumers also has a high position. Innovation should not be taken as more and more intensive and extensive research in the *status-quo* of consumer. No amount of quantitative analysis of consumer motivation or market segment or quantification can be said to be real alternative of innovation.

Innovation, therefore, seems to come more from internal thinking daring and dynamism than analysing the industry in Two by Two matrix in mind numbering detail.

CONCLUSION

I wish to point out at this stage that students and teachers of marketing should develop a technique of marketing forecast to foresee or have understanding and perception of what marketing in India in 200 AD and after would demand of them. We find that the need to understand consumer behaviour in the Indian context leads the rest of things behind; assessing the relative effectiveness of different forms of marketing inputs on a cost benefit equation. Conventionally marketers have always tended to think of most marketing inputs (other than the soft area of Advertising) as fairly measurable in terms of sales response. Every company has its own rules of thumb developed over the years from their own or their international affiliates based on experiences on how much is desirable to spend on promotions, distributions, product launched, or percentage of sales required to sustain market shares of stable ongoing brands, and so on. In the changed situation the question obviously is whether the old rule will be valid in changing context and how far such rules will apply in the changed situation. Here then is a rich area for constructive and continuous collaboration in research between the thinking manager and the user-friendly academics. This theme had any echoes in the interaction we have had with managers over the past few months and at various seminars.

I approach this august body that to perpetuate the memory of the learned academicians, a new marketing strategy by developed by them for the Indian Producers to be successful in the global market. Once again I thank you for the opportunity given to me.

Notes and References

1. *Times of India*, Patna May 8, 1994.
2. F.A. Mehta, Chairman, Forbes Group, Business India, June 1994.
3. UNCTAD Report 1994, Quoted in *Hindustan Times*, Sept. 17, 1994.
4. Will Indian brands Survive—A Survey Report, A & M, Oct. 1993, p. 51.
5. Chander, M. Sethi, Vice President Reckitt and Colman—Interview, June 1994.
6. *Hindustan Times*, Patna, 15th Sept., 1994.

7. Titoo Ahluwalia, Chairman Marketing and Research Group, A & M, June, 1993.
8. A & M, June 94.
9. Report of National Council of Applied Economic Research, 1993-94, New Delhi.
10. Business India, April-May, 1994, p. 68.
11. Export Reaching for the Skies, Business India, Oct. 9, 1994, pp. 57-59.

4

*Sustainable Human Development—Dimensions, Challenges and Policy Orientations**

B.P. SINGH**

I must place on record my deep sense of gratitude and delight having been invited by the Indian Commerce Association to deliver Prof. B.C. Tandon Memorial Lecture. Prof. Bharat Chandra was born on 22nd June, 1933 at Allahabad. He obtained his Master of Commerce Degree with First Division in 1952 from the University of Allahabad. He was awarded D. Litt. Degree of the same University in 1974 on his thesis "Pattern and Technique of India's Economic Development".

His teaching career primarily made a root at the University of Allahabad from October, 1953, though he served for a few months at D.N. College, Jabalpur which

* The present paper is the full text of the lecture delivered by Dr. Singh in the memory of Prof. B.C. Tandon.

** Head and Dean, Faculty of Commerce and Business, Delhi School of Economics, University of Delhi, Delhi.

was then affiliated to Sagar University, Sagar.

In 1971 Dr. B.C. Tandon was appointed Reader at the University of Allahabad. He was later made Director, Directorate of Correspondence Courses in 1978 in the same University.

Later, he moved to the Kurukshetra University as professor and Head, Department of Commerce in August, 1978. However, Kurukshetra was not destined to have him for long. In September, 1979 Prof. B.C. Tandon was invited to join as a Professor in the Faculty of Management Studies, University of Delhi, where he rose to the position of the Dean of the Faculty of Commerce and Business, Delhi School of Economics, University of Delhi.

Prof. Tandon has had authored about half a dozen books, besides getting his Doctoral Thesis published in two volumes. His valuable contributions were in the areas of Entrepreneurship, Economic Planning, Economic Development of Japan, and Research Methodology. Moreover, he had more than 30 research papers published in various National Journals and Magazines of repute.

During his academic career spanning over four decades, he was instrumental in guiding about twenty research scholars leading to the award of Doctoral Degree of the Universities of Allahabad, Kurukshetra, and Delhi. I had the privilege of being his student at the post-graduate level at the University of Allahabad from mid-1956 to mid-1958. Later on our association grew from strength to strength, and I always treated him as my friend, philosopher, and guide. It would be no exaggeration to say that in his sad demise I have lost elder brother, a loss which is not only irreparable for me personally but to the whole academic community. In the death of Prof. Tandon, the university community has lost an eminent Scholar, a distinguished colleague, and a very warm-hearted human being known for his love for colleagues and for students. In fact, Prof. Tandon was a unique personification of gentlemanliness, courtesy, and sophistication.

As a humble office-bearer of this great organization —Indian Commerce Association-I have a feeling that the ICA has maintained a lofty and rich tradition of arranging memorial lecture in the memory of such distinguished personalities of the academic community, with whom commerce education was a matter of faith and conviction. On my part, I feel honoured for having been called upon to perform this distinguished and noble task for the second tie by the ICA, on the earlier occasion it was in the memory of our distinguished son of the soil Prof. V.K.R.V. Rao for which I am indeed grateful to the Indian Commerce Association in general and to its office-bearers and the honourable members of the executive committee in particular.

The theme chosen for Prof. B.C. Tandon Memorial lecture is "Sustainable Human Development: Dimensions, Challenges and Policy Orientations", which in my opinion is a befitting tribute to the departed soul. Keeping in view his areas of advanced interests in Economic Planning, Entrepreneurship and Government and Business Interface.

CONCEPT OF SUSTAINABLE DEVELOPMENT

Human-beings, all the world over, are born with certain potential capabilities. The purpose of development is to create an environment in which all people can expand their capabilities, and opportunities could be enlarged for both present and future generations. The real foundation of human development is Universalism in acknowledging the life claims of everyone.

The paradigm of Sustainable human development values human life for itself. Development must enable all individuals irrespective of their class, caste, creed, sex, religion, language, or region to enlarge their human capabilities to the fullest and to put those capabilities to the best use in all fields of economic, social, cultural, and political.

Universalism of life claims is the common thread that binds the demands of human development today with the exigencies of development tomorrow, especially, with the need for environmental preservation and regeneration for the future.

Human development and sustainability are thus essential components of the same ethic of Universalism of life claims. There is no conflict or tension between the two concepts, for they are a part of the same overall design. In such conceptual framework, sustainability is, in a very broad sense, a matter of distributional equality of sharing development opportunities between present and future generations. The ethic of universalism clearly demands both intragenerational equity and intergenerational equity.

This equity is, however, in opportunities—not necessarily in final achievements. Each individual is entitled to a just opportunity to make the best use of his or her potential capabilities. So is each generation. How they actually use these opportunities, and the results they achieve, are a matter of their own choice. But they must have such a choice-now and in the future.

This Universalism of life claims a powerful idea that provides the philosophical foundations for many contemporary policies underlies the search for meeting basic human needs. It visualises a world where no child goes without education, where no human being is denied health care ad where all people can develop their potential capabilities. Universalism implies the empowerment of people. It protects all basic human rights; economic and social as well as civil and political, and it holds that the right to food is as sacrosanct as the right to vote. It demands no discrimination between all people, irrespective of gender, and religion.

Universalism advocates equality of opportunity, not equality of income though in a civilised society a basic minimum income should be guaranteed to everyone.

The basic thought of universalism of life claims in the contemporary world comes from pioneers like Mary Wollstonecraft (A vindication of the Right of Women, Published in 1972) and her friend Thomas Paine in the same year published the second part of the Rights of Man. Both were concerned with giving everyone—women and men power over their lives and opportunities to live according to their own values and aspirations.

HISTORICAL PERSPECTIVE

Interest in the concept of human development is not new, nor are the concerns of Sustainability. Today's belated return to human development means reclaiming an old and established heritage rather than importing or implanting a new diversion. The roots of the concept of human development can often be traced to early periods in human history and can be found in many cultures and religions. Aristotle wrote that "Wealth is evidently not the good we are seeking, for it is merely useful and for the sake of something else". A similar strain was reflected in the writings of early founders of political economy (Adam Smith, T.R. Malthus, Karl Marx and J.S. Mill). Adam Smith, the apostle of free-enterprise and private initiative, showed his concern that "economic development should enable a person to mix freely with others without being ashamed to appear in public"; he was expressing a concept of poverty that went beyond counting calories—a concept that integrated the poor into the main stream of the community.

Only during the twentieth century did the Social Sciences became increasingly concerned with economics—and economics with wealth rather than with the people, with the economy rather than with the society, with the maximisation of income rather than with the expansion of opportunities for people.

OPULANCE AND HUMAN DEVELOPMENT

Why should there be a tension between wealth maximization and human development? Is not the former indispensable for the latter? Wealth is important for good human life, but to concentrate on it to the neglect of human-being is ill-concerned and misplaced in terms of priorities for two important reasons.

First, accumulating wealth is not necessary for the fulfilment of some human choices. In fact, individuals and societies make any choices that require no wealth worth its name. A society does not have to be rich to be able to afford democracy. A family does not be wealthy to respect the rights of each member. A nation does not have to be affluent to treat women and men equally. Valuable social and cultural tradition can be largely independent of the people's wealth.

Second, human choices extend far beyond economic well-being. Human beings do need income/wealth, but they also want to enjoy long and healthy lives, drink deep at the fountain of knowledge, participate freely in the life of their community, breathe fresh air and enjoy the simple pleasures of life in a clean physical environment, and value peace of mind that comes from security in their homes, in their jobs, and in their society.

National wealth might expand people's choices, but it may not necessarily do so. The use that nations make of their wealth, not wealth itself, is decisive. And unless societies recognise that their real wealth is their people, an excessive obsession with the creation of material wealth can obscure the ultimate objective of enriching human lives.

The tension between wealth maximization and human development is not merely academic,it is real. Although there is definite correlation between material wealth and human well-being, but they need not necessarily move in the same direction. Many countries have a high GNP per-capita, but low human development indicators and *vice versa.* Countries at more or less similar levels of GNP per-capita may have vastly different human development indicators, depending on the use they have made of their national wealth. (See the table given below).

Similar Income, different HDI, 1991/92

Country	*GNP per capita (US $)*	*HDI value*	*HDI rank*	*Life expectancy (Years)*	*Adult literacy (%)*	*Infant (per, 1000 (live births)*
GNP per capita around $ 400 to $ 500						
Sri Lanka	500	0.665	90	71.2	89	24
Nicaragua	400	0.583	106	65.4	78	53
Pakistan	400	0.393	132	58.3	36	99
Guinea	500	0.191	173	43.9	27	135
GNP per capita around $ 1,000 to $ 1,100						
Ecuador	1010	0.718	74	66.2	87	58
Jordan	1060	0.628	98	67.3	82	37
El Salvador	1090	0.543	112	65.2	75	46
Congo	1040	0.461	123	51.7	59	83
GNP per capita around $ 2,300 to 2,600						
Chile	2360	0.848	38	71.9	94	17
Malaysia	2520	0.794	57	70.4	80	14
South Africa	2540	0.650	93	62.2	80	53
Iraq	2550	0.614	100	65.7	63	59

Recent studies confirm that even when inter-country data show a generally positive and statistically significant relationship between GNP per-head and indicators of quality of life, much of that relationship depends on the use of extra income for improving public education and health and for reducing absolute poverty.

In simple terms, it is not the level of income alone that matters—it is also the use that is made of this income. A society can spend its income on arms or on education. An individual can spend his or her income on narcotic drugs or on essential food. What is decisive is not the process of wealth maximisation but the choices that individuals and societies make-a simple truth often forgotten.

CONFUSION BETWEEN 'ENDS' AND 'MEANS'

It is often argued, and rightly so, that investing in people increases their productivity. It is then argued, and wrongfully so, that human development simply means HRD—increasing human capital. This formulation confuses ends and means. People are not merely instruments for producing commodities and services. And the purpose of development is not merely to produce more value-added irrespective of its use. Bestowing value on a human life only to the extent that it produces profits —the human capital approach—has obvious dangers. In its extreme form, it can easily lead to slave labour camps, forced child labour, and the exploitation of workers by management—as was the case during and after the industrial revolution.

Human development approach disapproves this excessive concentration on people as human capital. It favours and welcomes the central role of human capital in enhancing human productivity. But it is also equally concerned with creating the economic and political environment in which people can expand their human capabilities and use them appropriately. At the same time, it emphasises human choices that go far beyond economic well-being. It is well to remember Immanuel Kant's injunction "to treat humanity as and end withal, never as means only". the quality of human life is an end.

DIMENSIONS OF SUSTAINABLE DEVELOPMENT

Sustainable human development implies that we have a moral obligation to do atleast as well for our successor generations as our predecessors did for us. It means that current consumption cannot be financed for long by incurring economic debts that others must repay. It also implies that sufficient investment must be made in education and health of today's population so as not to create a social debt for future generations. Further, it entails that resources must be used in ways that do not create ecological debts by over exploiting the carrying and productive capacity of the earth. All postponed debts mortgage sustainability—whether economic debts, social debts or ecological debts. These debts rob coming generations of their legitimate options. That is whey the strategy for sustainable human development is to replenish all capita—physical, human and natural so that it maintains the capacity of the future generations to meet their needs atleast at the same level as that of the present generations.

SUSTAINABILITY AND ENVIRONMENT

There is no reason to accept the present way in which rich and poor nations share the common heritage of mankind. The North has roughly one-fifth of the world's population and four-fifth of its income, and it consumes 70% of the world's energy 75% of its metals, and 85% of its wood. If the eco-sphere were fully priced, not free, such consumption patterns could not continue. Had the environment been properly priced and tradable permits were issued to all nations (50% on the basis of GDP and 50% on the basis of population), the rich nations might have to transfer as much as 5% of their combined GDP to the poor nations.

The close link between global poverty and global sustainability will also have to be analysed carefully if the concept of sustainable development is to have any real meaning. The very poor, struggling for their daily survival, often lack the resources to avoid degrading their environment. In poor societies, what is at risk is not the quality of life—but life itself.

The poor are not preoccupied with loud emergencies of global warming or the depletion of the ozone layer. They are preoccupied with the silent emergencies—polluted water or degraded land—that put their lives and their livelihoods at risk. Unless the problems of poverty are addressed, environmental sustainability cannot be guaranteed.

Redistributing resources to the poor by improving their health, education, and nutrition is intrinsically important because it enhances their capabilities to lead more fulfilling lives. By increasing their human capital, it also has a lasting influence on their productivity and the ability to generate higher incomes—now and in the future.

Since the accumulation of human capital can replace some forms of exhaustible resources, human development should be seen a major contribution to sustainability. Development patterns that perpetuate today's inequities are neither sustainable nor worth sustaining.

SUSTAINABILITY AND POLICY ORIENTATION

Sustainability needs to be ensured in all sectors of the economy and at all levels of development process. It would require far-reaching chances in both national and global policy orientations.

At the national level, new balances must be struck between the efficiency of competitive markets, the legal and regulatory frameworks, the investments to enhance the capabilities of all, and the provision of social safety-nets for those with unequal access to the markets.

Balances between the compulsions of todays and the needs of tomorrow, between private imitative and public action, between individual greed and social compassion are solely needed for this purpose.

The essence of sustainable human development strategies must ensure a sustainable livelihood for all. These strategies—especially at the national level will thus have to focus on three core areas.

Poverty reduction;
Employment relation; and
Social Integration.

The detailed action programme areas have been listed here below in boxes 1.1 and 1.2.

Box 1.1

Poverty Reduction

Poverty is the greatest threat to political stability, social cohesion and the environmental health of the planet. Strategies for poverty reduction will certainly embrace all aspects of national policy. Some key lessons of country experience.

Basic Social Service—The state must help ensure a widespread distribution of basic social services to the poor, particularly basic education and primary health care.

Agrarian Reform—Since a large part of povetry in developing countries is concentrated in the rural areas, poverty reduction strategies often require a more equitable distribution of land and agricultural resources.

Credit for All—One of the most powerful ways of opening markets to the poor is to ensure more equal access to credit. The criteria of creditworthiness must change, and credit institutions must be decentralized.

Employment—The best way to extend the benefits of growth to the poor and to involve them in the expansion of output is to rapidly expand productive employment opportunities and to create a framework for ensuring a sustainable livelihood for everyone.

Participation—Any viable strategy for poverty reduction must be decentralized and participatory. The poor cannot benefit from economic development if they do not even participate in its design.

A Social Safety Net—Every country needs an adequate social safety net to catch those whom markets exclude.

Economic Growth—The focus of development efforts, in addition to increasing overall productivity, must be to increase the productivity of the poor. This will help ensure that the poor not only benefit from, but also contribute to, economic growth.

Sustainability—Poverty reduces, people's capacity to use resources in a sustainable manner, intensifying pressures on the ecosystem. To ensure sustainability, the content of growth must change-becoming less material-intensive and energy-intensive and more equitable in its distribution.

Box 1.2

Employment Creation

Creating sufficient opportunities for productive employment and sustainable livelihoods is one of the most important and most difficult tasks in any society. Based on experience, the central elements of an effective national employment strategy are likely to include:

Educational and Skills—To compete in a fast-changing global economy, every country has to invest heavily in the education, training and skill formation of its people.

An enabling Environment—Most new employment opportunities are likely to be generated by the private sector. But markets cannot work effectively unless governments create an enabling environment—including fair and stable macroeconomic policies, an equitable legal framework, sufficient physical infrastructure and an adequate system of incentives for private investment.

Access to Assets—A more equitable distribution of physical assets (land) and better access to means of production and credit information) are often essential to ensure sustainable livelihoods.

Labour—Intensive technologies—Developing countries have to be able to make the most efficient use of their factors of production to exploit comparative advantage of abundant labour. Tax and price policies should, where appropriate, try to encourage labour-intensive employment.

Public Works Programmes—Where private markets consistently fail to produce sufficient jobs, in certain regions or at certain times of the year, it may be necessary for the state to offer employment through public works programmes to enable people to survive.

Disadvantaged Groups—Where markets tend to discriminate against particular groups, such as women or certain ethnic groups, the state may need to consider targeted interventions or programmes of affirmative action.

Job-sharing—With the growing phenomenon of "jobless growth", it has become necessary to rethink the concept of work and to consider more innovative and flexible working arrangements including job sharing.

5

*The Interest Rate Muddle**

OM PRAKASH**

1. PROLOGUE

Lighthouses of Learning

Anyadevahurvidyaya Anyadahurvidyaya (;)

Iti Shursrum Dhiranam Ye Nastdwichchakshire (.)

—*Isha Upanishad*

(The wise and the learned who have attained spiritual knowledge have told and explained to us that knowledge of the Spirit has its own use quite different from that of the matter. We must all make use of both with the assistance of those who are well versed in spiritual knowledge as well as of those who are versed in the knowledge of material sciences).

* The present paper is the full text of the lecture delivered by Prof. Om Prakash in the memory of Prof. M.K. Ghose and Prof. S.P. Vijay Saradhi.

** Former Vice Chancellor, University of Rajasthan, Jaipur, and First National Fellow in Commerce.

I am grateful to the authorities of Kakatiya University for inviting me to deliver this Memorial Lecture. It was my privilege to have delivered the inaugural address at the celebrated UGC-sponsored National Seminar on Nehru and Planning of the Seminar Hall, Humanities Building, Kakatiya University, Warangal (Andhra Pradesh) on January 31, 1987, when the Technical Session on Achievements in Planning was also chaired by me. Now, it is a matter of great gratification that the dynamic Department of Commerce and Business Management in the youthful University is celebrating its Silver Jubilee, the threshold of adulthood. Again, it is a happy coincidence that Prof. A. Shankaraiah, who was then (January 1987) the Head of the Department and convener of such a prestigious Seminar, is now (December 1994) the Registrar, a key functionary of the entire University, as also the Conference Secretary of a major academic event like the XLVIII All-India Commerce Conference.

At the outset, let me pay my homage to the late Prof. S.P. Vijay Saradhi, who laid the solid foundation of Commerce and Management Education at Warangal, and lent lustre to Kakatiya University. I have had the pleasure of professional association with him on Boards to evaluate D.Litt. theses and to conduct *Viva Voce* Examinations. He had the capability to combine spiritual knowledge with the more material dimensions of the discipline of Commerce and Management Science in the midst of modern paradigms and their numerous manifestation.

I also take this opportunity of eulogising the late Prof. Mohit Kumar Ghosh, my great Guru and the first Professor/Head of the Department of Commerce (and Business Administration) at the University of Allahabad. In fact, his powerful critique of the cheap money policy was responsible for promoting my academic interest in interest rates as his student followed by an inspiring interaction during the decade I had the good fortune of being his younger colleague at the University of Allahabad. Prof. Ghosh was the founder of the Indian Commerce

Association, and it was my rare privilege to have been associated with him in the task of promotion well before its first Annual Conference held in 1947. But that is not all. He was an embodiment of objectivity, fairness and transparency in administration. I referred to his sterling attributes at some length on December 31, 1985, while delivering the Memorial Lecture in his honour on "Human Resource Management for the 21st Century: A case for "Open Management" on the occasion of the XXXIX All India Commerce Conference at Banaras Hindu University, Varanasi.[1] More recently, on September 9, 1994, I delivered his Centenary Lecture on Indian Business Under Multinational siege at the Motilal Nehru Institute of Research and Business Administration, University of Allahabad. Though a lot more can be said about such Lighthouses of Learning, I would like to conclude this prologue with what I saw on placards in October 1993 during the course of my visit to Sewagram (Wardha), the Asram so closely connected with Mahatma Gandhi and India's freedom struggle. It is imperative to sheer clear of:

(i) Politics without Principles;
(ii) Wealth without Work;
(iii) Commerce without Morality;
(iv) Education without Character;
(v) Pleasure without conscience; and
(vi) Worship without Sacrifice.

2. INTEREST RATES

The Indian Antiquity

One the basis of socio-economic considerations, a manifestly differential structure of interest rates was stipulated by Manu, the great Hindu law-giver and by some other authors of ancient Indian scriptures. According to Kautilya's Arthasastra an interest of a pana and a quarter per month per cent (15% per annum) was considered just on ordinary debts. The commercial lending rate, known as Vyavkarika, was five panas per month per cent (60% per annum). That is, it was four times the basic lending rate. When merchants took special risks, the interest rate was still higher. It was 10 panas per month per cent (120% per annum) when the merchandise passed through forest areas, and 20 panas per month per cent (240% per annum) in the case of sea voyages. Sometimes, the rate of interest was mutually arranged between the concerned parties, irrespective of governmental prescriptions, as indicated by Yajnavalkya, another authority on ancient India. In any case, "the rate of interest was high as we can gather from these texts and this has caused scholars to suggest that the country was short of capital."[2] This can also be interpreted to mean that commercial adventures in ancient India, notwithstanding a high element of risk, were both popular and profitable. That is, the business community was quite enterprising. Some traces of this phenomenon were found in Jaipur State even at the time of its integration into Rajasthan after the attainment of Indian independence. Under the 'Sawai' system, a borrower of one rupee in the morning has to repay a rupee and a quarter in the evening (or the next morning). Thus, the rate of interest was no less than 25 per cent per day (say, even without compounding, 750% per month or 9000% per year).

All the same, the governmental prerogative to prescribe banking norms was well recognised in ancient India. According to Kautilya, "Interest on debts due from persons who are engaged in sacrifices taking a long time, or who are suffering from disease, or who are detained in the houses of their teachers (for learning), or who are either minors or too poor, shall not accumulate."[3] The structure of regulation designed for debts was made applicable to deposits also, though deposit banking was not quite popular in ancient India. Ordinarily, the depositor was not entitled to claim any interest. However, certain inscriptions at Nasik indicate that an interest of 9 to 12 per cent was payable on deposits. Generally speaking, a moneylender was not supposed to make use of deposits for personal comfort, lending operations or other business. In the event of a violation of this norm, he was called upon to pay bhogavetnam compensation for use) to be determined after considering the circumstances of place and time, besides a fine of 12 panas. If there was loss in use, it had to be made good in addition to be a higher fine of 24 panas. In case the deposit was mortgaged, sold or lost, the banker had to restore four times its value, and to pay penalty of five times the stipulated value.

Thus, while charging high rates of interest on money lending activity was deemed legitimate, deposit banking in ancient India was quite close to (and, in certain respects, much more ginger than) what later appeared as the interest free concept of Islamic Banking. For example, the Islamic Development Bank was created in 1974 (as a Regional Development Bank) by the Organization of the Islamic Conference, to encourage economic growth in Muslim countries and communities. In view of the Koranic principle forbidding usury, it does not grant loans or credit for interest. Instead, it finances industrial development projects by holding equity capital or granting loans at a nominal 'commission' rate (just to cover administrative expenses). The Islamic Development Bank also extends loans to assist member countries in financing essential imports. According to F.R. Faridi, Islamic Economics does not permit any earning on the basis of financial manipulation, while the treatment of capital as an instrument of profit leaves only one option to increase one's wealth by real production.[4] Summarising ten results of Hindu Economics, M.G. Bokare lists Interest-free Economy (Islamic principle subsumed) and Exploitationless Economy (Socialism sub-sumed) at fourth and fifth serial numbers, respectively.[5]

3. INTERESTS RATES

The Current Muddle

The last six decades since the passage of the Reserve Bank of India Act, 1934, can be divided into three periods of roughly two decades each. The first two decades could pass as a period of cheap money and relatively low price level, notwithstanding the inflationary impact of the Second World War (1939-45). The Bank Rate (standard rate at which the Reserve Bank of India is prepared to buy or rediscount bills of exchange or other commercial papers eligible for purchase)—which now seems to have gone into the oblivion—was kept pegged at as low as three per cent for no less than sixteen years (1935-51). In fact, during the First Five Year Plan (1951-56), the general price level actually declined. During the next two decades, both inflation and interest rates looked up at 'walking' speed. The average rate of interest on Government securities went up from 3.75 per cent in 1955-56 to 6.04 per cent in 1975-76. In the wake of oil boom ignited by the OPEC pricing policy initiated in 1973, inflation went up at 'jogging' speed during the last two decades (1974-1994) notwithstanding occasional deviations. The high waterwark of short-term (commercial) and long-term (industrial) lending rates since 1980 is revealed by the following Table 5.1.[6]

The number of interest slabs on bank advances under wide-ranging strait-jacket regulations had gone up to 20 in 1989-90. Somehow, these were reduced to only three in 1993-94. Announcing the credit policy for the busy season (October 1994-March 1995), Dr. C. Rangarajan, the RBI Governor and my younger colleague at the University of Rajasthan (Jaipur), freed lending rates of scheduled commercial banks for credit limits over two lakhs of rupees. However, interest rates for term loans and all other advances up Rs. 25,000 were still regulated at the erstwhile rate of 12%, while interest rate for loans between Rs. 25,000 and two lakhs of rupees was brought

TABLE 5.1

Nominal Interest (Lending) Rates in India

Short-term	*Long-term*
(i) July 1980, 19.4% (Ceiling)	(i) 1980-81, 14%
(ii) April 1985, 17.5% (Do)	(ii) 1985-86, 14%
(iii) September 1990, 16% (Floor)	(iii) 1989-90, 14%
(iv) April 1991, 17% (Do)	(iv) 1990-91, 14-15%
(v) July 1991, 18.5% (Do)	(v) August 1991, 18-20%
(vi) October 1991, 20% (Do)	(vi) October 1991, 18.5-20.5%
(vii) May 1992, 19% (Do)	(vii) November 1992, 17.5%-19.5%
(viii) October 1992, 18% (Do)	(viii) March 1993, 17-19%
(ix) March, 1992, 17% (Do)	(ix) August 1993, 16.5-18.5%
(x) June 1993, 16% (Do)	(x) September 1993, 15.5-18.5%
(xi) September 1993, 15% (Do)	(xi) 1993-94 Range (14-17%) IDBI's Long-term Prime Rate (LTPR) 14.6%
(xii) October 18, 1994 (Partial Deregulation) State Bank of India's Prime Lending Rate, 14% (Excluding Interest Tax)	(xii) December 1, 1994 to May 1995 IDBI's LTPR 14% (Including Interest Tax)

down marginally from 14% to 13.5%. This implied, in practice, a back-door regulation of commercial lending rate (a floor rate of 13.5%) for bigger loans. The SBI Chairman Mr. Dipak Basu, opined in this context: "I don't think this will lead to a significant additional demand for credit".[7] The irony appears to be that there is enough credit within the country, but it is quite expansive; and, even a marginal reduction in the commercial lending rate seem to have made some Banks nervous regarding their viability.

Another contradiction has been the existence of palpably low rates of interest for agriculture/certain priority sectors, such as four percent under the Differential Interest Rate Scheme. Even though the proportion of such concessonal credit tended to be low, it gave the Banks an excuse for low profitability/losses. While inaugurating the 54th Annual Conference of the

Indian Society for Agricultural Economics at Shivaji University (Kolhapur) on November 26, 1994, Dr. Manmohan Singh, the Finance Minister and my younger colleague at the Punjab University (Chandigarh), opined that India's agricultural credit system had been seriously weakened by excessively subsidised interest rates, the culture of non-recovery and persistent expectation of write-offs.

From the standpoint of depositors too, interest rates in India have presented a muddled state of affairs. First, interest on term deposits did not rise *pari passu* with the upward movement in commercial lending rates, so that the gap widened from the norm of two to as much as seven (20 minus 13=7) per cent. With effect from October 18, 1994, 10% is the rigid maximum rate which banks can pay on term deposits, while 14% is the practical minimum above which they can charge any rate on commercial lending operations. Secondly, even within the ceiling of 10%, there are anomalies. For example, the ICICI Bank (a newly established commercial bank) announced an interest of only eight per cent for deposits of over two years, as against 10% on deposits for 91 days to two years. With some variations, other Banks had similar anomalies. As such, few would like to block their funds for more than 91 days (in the case of ICICI Bank). Thirdly, with annual inflation rate running around 10 per cent (9.69%, provisionally estimated for the week ending November 26, 1994), the real interest rate is nearly nil (zero) even at the maximum permissible rate for term deposits in Banks. For the usual six, seven or even eight per cent deposits, the real interest rate is surely in negative (minus). Fourthly, in respect of Savings Bank Accounts, the rate of interest was enhanced from 5 per cent to 6 per cent early in 1993, only to be reduced to the same 5% later during that very year. With effect from November 1, 1994 this rate has been further reduced to 4.5%, which, in real terms, amounts to minus (—)5.5%. Fifthly, the rate of interest on monthly income schemes of the Unit Trust of India has been reduced from 14% to

12% during the last two years. Besides that, assured interest is now provided for only one year (after which it can be reduced to any level, even zero) as against five to seven years in earlier schemes. Contrary to its magnificent record of credibility, the UTI failed to honour its own announcement of 13% in he UTI Bulletin for a monthly income scheme to be introduced in October 1994. The scheme was deferred to November/December 1994 with a reduced rate of 12% interest, and that, too, assured for one year only. There is a move to cut even the 12% interest on Public Provident Fund Accounts. All this goes against genuine investors, particularly retired persons, widows and others depending for their livelihood on past savings. They are being doubly punished on account of inflation as well as reduced rates of interest. In fine, almost all the "investors" (as distinguished from 'speculators') are being pushed into the rings of stock exchanges and other highly hazardous adventures where 'lambs' can hardly escape crucification.

What can be a pertinent paradigm for short-term *vis-a-vis* long-term rates of interest? According to the Liquidity Preference Theory, the latter should be higher than the former as a rational relationship. But, the usual pattern in India since 1948, when the first public sector development bank (IFCI) became operational after the attainment of independence, has been to keep interest rates on term loans lower than the commercial lending rate.[8] This was, basically, to encourage investment in fixed assets. However, the same logic worked the other way for long-term depositors who were, generally, offered higher rates of interest than those on short-term deposits Savings Bank Accounts (while Current Account holders were, often, not given any interest, or even asked to pay some incidental charge). This dichotomy did reduce the bakers' margin in respect of interest rates applicable to long-term transactions. But, the same had to be endured for two operational reasons. First, if the interest on long-term deposits is lower than threat on short-term deposits, the depositors would, normally, prefer to get short-term deposits extended from time to time. Secondly, if the long-term lending rate is higher than the commercial lending rate, borrowers might prefer to get sort-term loans renewed from time to time (although this may not be operationally so feasible as the renewal of deposits).

Regarding the interfáce between inflation and interest rates, the completion tended to be positive in the early stages of India's Economic Liberalisation Programme (Reforms) initiated in 1991. However, in a comment by a Head of Investment Economics at American Express Bank Ltd., on "The Vanishing Equity Premium it has been recently suggested that "Investors now know that, even in peacetime modern democratic States are quite capable of allowing inflation and low short-term interest rates to co-exist for long periods. Such a realisation implies that the require return on bonds should be higher than in the 1950's to reflect the risk of unanticipated inflation. This could imply that the yield curve should be steeper, which is indeed why we have seen in the United States in the last two years."[9] Table 5.2 goes indicate that real interest rates (three-month money market) in the USA were much lower than those in many other developed countries:[10]

If nominal interest rates in India, as given in Table 5.1, are converted into real interest rates with the

TABLE 5.2

Real Interest Rates in Developed Economics (1993)

S.No.	Country	Downward (D)/ Upward (U)	Range
(i)	Denmark	(D)	6-7%
(ii)	Spain	(U)	4-5%
(iii)	Italy	(U)	4-5%
(iv)	France	(D)	4-5%
(v)	Holland	(D)	4-5%
(vi)	Germany	(D)	2-3%
(vii)	Britain	(U)	2-3%
(viii)	USA	(U)	0-1%
(ix)	Japan	(D)	0-1%

annual rate of inflation as the deflator, and then compared with real interest rates in Japan and the USA (or Britain and Germany), there may not be much of disparity. Yet, there is a gulf of difference between a situation of 14% interest with 13% inflation and another one of four per cent interest with three per cent inflation. When, on November 16, 1994, the US Federal Reserve raised the discount rate it charges banks for loans form 4.00 to 4.75 per cent (a rise of just three-quarters of a percentage), it was termed as the boldest attempt on inflation in thirteen years, it was the biggest increase since May 1981 when, in the context of a double-digit rate of inflation, the discount rate was raised from 13 to 14 per cent. As against this, a cut in interest rates by one per cent (or so) in India with effect from October 18, 1994 has hardly caused a ripple. Traditionally, there has been a low level of sensitivity on this score in India. And, of late, the claims made by the government in this regard, and the motives behind policy moves, have been looked upon with the great deal of suspicion. For example, the frequent assertion that inflation in India has been reduced from 17% to less than 10% by the Government which took office in June 1991 is not correct. When Mr. P.V. Narasimha Rao assumed office as Prime Minister, and Dr. Man Mohan Singh as Finance Minister, in June 1991, the annual inflation rate was about 10%; and, so it is after they have been in office for three-and-a-half years. The inflation rate rose to some 17% as a result of the new Governments' policies (in particular, devaluation). Actually, the target was to roll back prices to the level obtaining one year back. As such, the Wholesale Price Index (1981-82=100), which stood at 198.4 for June 1991, should have been brought down to 176.9 (obtaining in June 1990). Far from that, the WPI stood as high as 275.2 for the week ending November 26, 1994, representing an increase of some 38% since June 1991, and of about 55% over the June 1990 level.

Thus the interest-rate policy of the Government of India in recent years has failed to control inflation. Again, as Dr. Amartya Sen, Lamount Professor at Harvard University and President of the American Economic Association, asserted in November 1994 at the John Hopkins University School of International Studies, "The story that India's growth has picked up is wrong"; Well, if neither of the two major objectives (control of inflation and promotion of economic growth) has been served, does it not mean that the frequent changes in interest rates brought about in India, particularly during 1991-94, represent a 'muddled' state of affairs?

4. EPILOGUE

Conclusions

The glaring and persistent disparity between nominal and real interest rates calls for a reduction in price inflation rate to zero in order and genuine investor may have a fair deal.

Frequent and marginal changes in interest rates only add to accounting complications without achieving any of the major objectives, such as control of inflation and promotion of economic growth, set for themselves by developing countries like India. Even in the case of developed economies, 'fine tuning' may fail to work.

The gap between the commercial lending rate and the maximum interest available on term deposits needs to be narrowed down to two per cent or so by cutting down administrative costs and promoting operational efficiency of banks/financial institutions which should steer clear of frenzied speculation and other questionable practices that have come to light in the context of the 1992 stock exchange scam.

The interest rate on provident funds, in the current context, should not be lowered. Moreover, monthly income schemes should provide guaranteed return for the next five years or so in order that senior citizens and others depending on past savings for their livelihood do not face embarrassment. The Finance Minister has been kind to senior citizens in providing income tax concessions. But these do not mean much specially for those who subsist below the taxation limit.

The tax on interest rates should be abolished. Such a levy, besides confusing calculations, has no place in a liberal economic system which the government have adopted as their watchword.

Genuine investor should be provided with adequate opportunities for investment which gives regular assured income besides protecting the real value of investments. In fine, wisdom seems to lie in keeping inflation low, real interest rates moderate, and some possibility of the principal amount appreciating in real terms.[11]

Independent academicians should have their rightful place in deliberations designed to decide interest rates and other important policy matters. It is a pity that the academic contribution of even Dr. B.R. Ambedkar, once a Professor at the Sydenham College of Commerce and Economics (Bombay), has been forgotten while there has been so much political focus on him during the last quinquennium. I am possibly, the only person in the country to have highlighted this dimension of his personality in my centenary lectures delivered in his honour at IIT (Bombay) and elsewhere. I have compared him with both Karl Marx and J.M. Keynes. For a decade (1913-23), both in term of the volume of work and its quality, Bhimrao Ramji Ambedkar set up unique records of contribution at Columbia University, the London School of Economics and elsewhere.

The academic virtues of such Lighthouses of Learning should not remain hidden. Let me close this Memorial Lecture in honour of the late Professor S.P. Vijay Saradhi of the Department of Commerce and Business Management, Kakatiya University (Warangal) and the late Professor M.K. Ghosh (of the University of Allahabad), founder of the Indian Commerce Association, with a couplet from the great Urdu poet, Akbar Allahabadi:

> *Nigahen kamilon Ki par Hi jati Hen Zamane Men:*
> *Kahin Chhipta He Akbar Phool Patton Men Nihan Hokar.*

Notes and References

1. Om Prakash, "Human Resource Management for the 21st Century: A Case for "Open Management" *Indian Journal of Commerce*, No. 146, January-Mach 1986 (Also, Om Prakash, "The Management Panorama, RBSA Publishers, Jaipur, 1990, pp. 1-16).
2. G.L. Adhya, "Early Indian Economic Studies in the Economic Life of Northern and Western India (200 BC-300 AD)", Asia Publishing House, Bombay, 1966, p. 100.
3. R. Shamasatry, "Kautilya's Arthasastra", Fourth Edition, Printed at Raghuvar Printing Press, Mysore, 1951, p. XXXII (Original Preface dated 20th November, 1914).
4. F.R. Farid, "Islamic Economics: An Alternative System", based on ideas as President, Indian Association for Islamic Economics at the first All-India Conference on Islamic Economics organised by IAIE (Karnataka Chapter on Jan. 27-28, 1993, at Bangaloe, *Southern Economist*, July 15, 1993.
5. M.G. Bokare, "Hindu Economics", Swadeshi Jagaran Manch, Published by Janaki Prakashan, New Delhi, 1993, p. 353. Reference may also be made to its (Bokare's) review by Abdul Aziz in *Southern Economist* (June 15, 1993) and another one by Om Prakash in *The Nagpur Times* (October 24, 1993).
6. *The Economic Times* (Bombay) of September 16, 1993: *The Economic Times* (New Delhi) of October 18, 1994; and *The Economic Times* (New Delhi) of November 30, 1994.
7. *The Economic Times* (New Delhi), Tuesday Interview, 6 December 1994.
8. The IDBI Chairman Mr. S.H. Khan, observed on October 19, 1994: "Traditionally long-term lending rates in India have been cheaper than short-term lending rates. This was done to boost industrial development. I don't see long-term rates moving up in the near future since the market is awash with surplus liquidity".
9. John Calverley in Richard O'Brien (Ed.), I, "Finance and the Intenrational Economy: The Economy, 7" Published by Oxford University Press, Inc., New York, for the Amex Bak Review, 1993.

10. "Wha hapened to inflation? Most governments are not exactly sure", *The Economist* (London), October 30-November 5th, 1993.

11. Om Prakash, "The Commercial Society", Westvill Publishing House, New Delhi, 1994, p. 86.

6

*Economic Liberalisation, Development and Quality of Human Life**

P.N. SINGH**

I express my deep sense of gratitutde to the Executive Committee of the Indian Commerce Association for giving me this opportunity to deliver lecture in the sacred memory of Late C.D. Singh, one of the past presidents of the Association. Born on the 14th 1927, Dr. Chandra Deo Singh passed his Matriculation Examination in 1943 and B.Com. Examination in 1948 from Patna University, Patna; and was placed in the First Division in both the Examinations. He did his M.Com. from B.H.U., Varanasi in 1950 and secured first class position in the University. He received his Ph.D. degree from Cornel (U.S.A.) in 1964 and D.Litt. in 1980.

Dr. Singh started his career as a teacher from H.D. Jain College, Arrah (Bihar) in 1950; and served Patna

* The present paper is the full text of the lecture delivered by Dr. Singh in the memory of Dr. C.D. Singh.

** Prof. and Head, University Department of Economics, B.R. Ambedkar Bihar University, Muzaffarpur.

University for some time. He became Reader in Bihar University in 1954, Professor in Bhagalpur University in 1965, and retired from there as Head and Dean on the 31st January 1989.

He served Magadh University, Bodh-Gaya as Pro-Vice-Chancellor from 1975 to 1977 and as Vice-Chancellor from 1977 to 1978. He was again tipped for the Vice-Chancellorship of L.N. Mithila University, Darbhanga in 1983 and he continued there till 1985. The University Grants Commission accorded recognition to his scholarship, experience and expertise by appointing him National Lecturer and Member of Panel of Commerce and Business Administration. As a distinguished teacher, he was associated with several academic bodies of different universities. He addressed All India Commerce Conference in Burdwan in 1988 as President of the Indian Commerce Assocation. He was one of the pioneers of this organisation of the teachers of Commerce, Economics and Management from the very beginning of his career as a teacher. He never missed an opportunity for attending the conference, contributing to the growth of knowledge, providing strength to the organisation and getting his inspiring presence felt.

Dr. C.D. Singh has authored nearly half a dozen books which are considered to be the valuable contributions in the fields of accounting, business administration, industrial relations and commerce education. He had written several research papers and articles which were published in noted national and international journals. He had to his credit of supervising four research works leading to the award of D.Litt. degrees and twenty-nine leading to the award of Ph.D. degrees of different Universities.

Dr. Singh was a magnetic personality, an intellectual giant, a distinguished teacher, a serious reseracher and thinker, a sincere friend, a perfect guide and a human being in the true sense of the term. He believed in high living and high thinking, marked with simplicity and humanity. He was a true lover of mankind and was loved and respected by all irrespective of caste, creed, religion and different age groups. I had a long association with him and I always treated him with reverence and regards as my father and guardian. In his sad demise I lost my guardian and this community of Commerce and Management teachers, its great academic leader. The Indian Commerce Associaton deserves all appreciation for maintaining a healthy and rich tradition of arranging lectures to perpetuate the memory of such a great soul and the distinguished personality of the academic community of such a great soul and the distinguished personality of the academic community with whom commerce education was a matter of faith and conviction, I feel honoured for having called upon to perform this noble task and for that I am grateful to the I.C.A. in general and the members of its Executive Committee in particular.

The theme chosen for Dr. C.D. Singh Memorial Lecture is "Economic Liberalisation, Development and Quality of Human Life". This topic is optical and at the same time a befitting tribute to the departed soul as Dr. Singh was very liberal in his manner and thinking, areas of his interest being planning development, industrial relations and human resource development.

In 1947 when Jawaharlal Nehru addressed to the Nation of their tryst with destiny, he promised that the main task ahead for the Government was to eliminate disease, hunger and ignorance. India's poor performances have darkened the country's economic prospects; sick and illiterate people do not make good works. But more important it demonstrates that governments have failed in the most basic way to improve the lives of their citizens. According to the World Bank, 63 per cent of India's population under five is malnourished. Perhaps, 40 per cent of the world's desperately poor live in India. Apart from a tiny elite in Delhi and Bombay, India's rich are poor by anybody else's standards; according to the National Council for Applied Economic Research only 2-3 per cent of the population has a household income of more than Rs. 78,000. Fewer than half of the people can read.

There are 184 countries in the world, each different from the other in its approach of whom there are the very rich and the highly developed yet others that have low income and are least developed. The trend in the post-war era made nations to follow three different economic systems free market economic system followed by Western Europe, America and Far Eastern Countries like Japan, Korea, Singapore, Malaysia Thailand, Hong Kong, Taiwan, etc. while another group of nations like USSR, Eastern Europe and China adopted socialistic and planned economic system; India of course adopted unique mixed economic system. The results of these economic philosophies in early nineties clearly indicated that market driven economic system have helped nations to grow faster, generate wealth and bring prosperity to their people. The socialist planned economic system virtually collapsed and made nations to adopt market driven economic systems. The mixed economic system in India despite an excellent beginning did not yield the desired results. Three decades ago India and South Korea were at similar stage of economic growth. Today the per capita income in Korea is ten times that of India's and its economy has witnessed an average annual growth of over 8 per cent compared to around 4 per cent of India.

The reasons for India losing this economic race are obvious. The Nehruvian policies in the sixties followed by Indira Gandhi's socialist ideas in the seventies ensured that Indian industry remained uncompetitive both domestically and internationally. This fostered inefficiency and unproductivity which had an adverse impact on growth rates. The value of goods produced by an Indian worker $ per hour averages $ 4.49 while the figures is $ 34.44 in case of a German worker. The average capacity utilisation of industries in India is 70 per cent as against 85 per cent and 95 per cent in Korea and Japan.

Our efforts at structural adjustment of the economy which we began in the midst of the unprecedented financial and fiscal crisis in mid-1991 was based on the tenet that our objective of self-reliant growth and social justice called for a change in attitude towards and the form of macro-economic management both in respect of current problems and basic economic structure. The rationale for the new economic policy stems from the logic of our own experience over the last four decades where the economy has not grown to its full potential where self-reliance is still a dream and adequate progress has not been made in the basic social indicators. It also derives from the example of countries in East and the South-East Asia, where in the ambit of a broad and by and large benign state regulation and sometimes intervention, enough initiative was given to economic agents which helped propel these economies from a level of underdevelopment not far different from ours to the ranks of newly industrialised countries.

Economic policy and structures have to be related to time and space. Way back in 1959, Mr. A.D. Shroff said:

> "We should cling passionately in democratic values, allow the fullest scope of individual initiative and enterprise, recognise the dignity and worth of the individual and place trust in him and thus bring about through democracy and free enterprise within socially desirable state regulation an area of plenty prosperity, freedom and social justice."

Following the world trend and recognising the strength in A.D. Shroff's philosophy Indian economy switched over from a controlled economy to a market oriented one. Though the policies of liberalisation, marketisation, privatisation and globalisation were initiated by Shri Rajiv Gandhi well back in 1985 these were accelerated in 1991 by the Government under the stewardship of Prime Minister P.V. Narasimha Rao. The major structural adjustment efforts aimed at improving the supply side of the national equation and at improving the competitive efficiency of the economy have, of course, been in the area of industry, trade and exchange policies.

It is now appropriate to evaluate and understand whether the policies have been able to accelerate the process of growth and whether these policies will ultimately achieve the economic and social objectives as laid down in our Constitution and enunciated time and again in our plan documents. Some people feel that there is still some scope for further action in industrial liberalisation and company legislation. The two major areas where the thrust of liberalisation has made little headway are agriculture and labour policy. Thus, there are conflicting views with regard to effectiveness of the new economic policy.

ECONOMIC DEVELOPMENT AND QUALITY OF HUMAN LIFE

The keys to effective economic development are equity, participation, self-reliance, sustainability and holistic approach to community life. The economic development is for the people and by the people. It is not other way round. One has to keep the people at the centre stage of development strategy which both market-led growth and state controlled growth strategy negate. The purpose of development is to create an environment in which all people can expand their capabilities and put them to the best use. Redistributing resources to the poor by improving their health, education and nutrition is very important because it enhances the capabilities of the people to lead more fulfilling lives. It also has a lasting influence on the productivity and the ability to generate higher incomes.

A developmental strategy that can lead to improvement in the quality of human life hinges on a concept of sustainable human development which details action plan in three directions: (i) poverty reduction, (ii) employment generation, and (iii) social integration. To enhance the quality of its human capital, India needs to invest more in health facilities—health costs in India are 1.5 per cent of the G.D.P. while the worldwide average is 9 per cent, ensure widespread of literacy, expand vocational training programmes and get companies to invest more in training and development. Simultaneously, investment in research should be encouraged; currently in India it is less than one per cent of sales as compared to 8 per cent in developed countries.

What is needed is people oriented development models. The essential elements of social production are reproduction of labour and agricultural development which determine the supply of wage goods, savings and investment which determine the future course of economic growth and the market which provides signal for organising production and using national-resources and technology.

Under the pressure of globalisation, governments are reducing expenditure on education and health, thus, retarding the growth of human capital. The growth of agriculture is relatively delinked from local people's requirement and oriented to export markets. Environment is degraded owing to general deregulation. Savings and investments are turned to the global requirement of trans-national capital. No realising these truths, big businesses pursue a model of development that makes them dependent and vulnerable to external debt, alien consumption pattern and military weapons on the one hand and condemns a vast mass of humanity to illiteracy and poverty on the other.

The people-oriented development model demands that agricultural workers, peasants, marginal and middle farmers and workers, small industrialists, etc. may be organised in a broad social group. A new economic programme should be designed to directly benefit them. This new economic progrmame must ensure the right to work and decent living for all citizens within a reasonable period of time. In order to increase job opportunities the state has to assume a more native role; because market mechanism may maximise profits but not employment. State Plans should be designed to fill up the infrastructural gaps in backward regions. This is the demand side of economics and politics for the poor as against the Reagon-Thatcher conception of the supply side. It counterpoised the people's right to reasonable living against globaliser's right to profit autocentric development, against dependent industrialisation to participative social democracy and against centralised rule. The model of autocentric development based on the demands on the side of economics is a humane and sustainable alternative to the ongoing disastrous process of globalisation.

Search for a just and sustainable system of production and distribution has never been so urgent as now. The economically deprived sections of the less developed countries who constitute the majority in their respective countries cannot endure the sufferings any longer. The world is beset with flagrant intentional inequality in the distribution of income, knowledge, power and wealth. Glaring ecological degradation is threatening the existence of life. Old systems have failed to rectify these problems. Capitalism and market system of organising economic life characteristically generate economic inequality and ecological imbalance. Under the impact of the globalising process, the governments are losing the human face. It has projected a new face of world capitalism-profit-oriented and anti-welfare state.

Nicholas Kaldor of Cambridge University, U.K. has described the economic performance of world capitalism over the period of 1950 to 1965 as a long secular boom.

By 1965 the capitalist system, had acquired new characteristics. The expansion of the trans-national and international financial institutions over the decade integrated national markets into the global market. This process of globalisation was reinforced by the last GATT agreement which covers a wide range of areas such as agriculture, investment, intellectual property rights, services, use of medicine, P.D.S., prices, subsidies, etc. The World Trade Organisation subjects the national economies to supernational control.

THE POST-REFORM SCENARIO

The economy has distinctively performed better in 1994-95 than in the proceeding three years under the New Economic Policy, however, the major problems remain unresolved. These may be listed as:

(a) Inflation, unemployment, growing inequality in income, rising number of people below the poverty line and relative deprivation.
(b) declining savings and investment rates;
(c) rising budget deficits;
(d) flow of hot money in the economy and instability in external accounts.

The positive features of the economy are-pick up in the rates of growth particularly in the industrial sector, record level of reserve of food grains and foreign exchange, high tax buoyancy and lower fiscal deficits. Our so-called structural adjustment programmes, globalisation and so on are designed to help export growth and reduction of unemployment of technologically industrialised countries suffering from acute recession. Out of total unemployment of 820 million in the world, unemployment in the developed countries is only 35 million and that in India it is more than 125 million. At home, out of 331 million work-force, the rural areas provide job opportunities to 220 million people and about 90 per cent of our workforce is in unorganised sector. Till today, there is no labour law to protect these unorganised workers. The Government godowns are overflowing with around 30 million tonnes of food grains, whereas more than half of the population is illiterate and living below the poverty line. Will the Government even open the gates of these godowns for these people so that everyone can go to bed with atleast one meal.

The year 1994-95 had the fastest growth rate in the last four years. After the crisis induced low growth rate of 0.9 per cent in 1991-92 the economy had responded to reform measures to record growth of 4.3 per cent in 1992-93 and 1993-94 and 5.3 per cent in 1994-95. The remarkable progress made by the Indian economy can be gauged by a few simple comparisons. Compared to overall economic growth of 0.9 per cent in 1991-92, the rate in 1994-95 was 5.3 per cent. Industrial production which virtually stagnated in 1991-92 has registered a growth rate of 8 per cent in 1994-95. Food grains production which had declined to 168 million tonnes in 1991-92 had attained a record high of 185 million tonnes in 1994-95.

Whereas the increase in the economy in total wide employment is estimated to have only about 3 million in 1991-92, an expansion of about 6 million is estimated for each of the year 1992-93 and 1993-94 with the prospect of a large rise in current year. The Central Government's fiscal deficits continue to be high and this is reflected in continuing inflationary pressure. The borrowing requirements of high fiscal deficits are a source of pressure on interest rates and adversely affect the availability of resources for productive investment. Table 6.1 gives an idea of the present state of the economy:

An important achievement of the post-reform period claimed by the Finance Minister is the reduction in trade deficits and the accumulation of foreign exchange reserves of the order of about $ 20 billion. This has restored the

TABLE 6.1

Economic Indicators Percentage Change over Previous Year

Particulars	*1991-92*	*1992-93*	*1993-94*	*1994-95*
G.D.P.	0.9	4.3	4.3	5.3
Agricultural Production	0.2	4.1	2.2	2.2
Industrial Production	0.6	2.3	4.1	8.0
Wholesale Price Index	13.6	7.0	10.8	11.5
Imports at Current Prices	19.4	15.7	18.2	18.6
Exports at Current Prices	35.3	21.9	29.5	17.3

Source: Economic Survey, 1994-95, Government of India.

credibility of India in the international market. A look at Table 6.2 reveals that the imports due to the policies of liberalisation have risen by 19.1 per cent in 1994-95 as against increase in exports at the rate of 12.3 per cent.

Secondly, in the pre-reform period, a part of the trade deficit was neutralised by a positive balance in the invisible account. Thirdly, the increase in foreign exchange reserves is not the result of any favourable balance on current account but is the consequence of unilateral flows in the form of external assistance from the World Bank, IMF or commercial borrowing or NRI deposits, etc.

Industrial Policy Statement of 1991 clearly stated, "in order to invite foreign investment in high priority industries requiring large investments and advanced technology, it has been decided to provide approval for direct foreign investment upto 51% foreign equity in such industries". The foreign collaborations approved during 1991-92 to December 1993 reveals that the priority sector accounts for about 61% of total foreign investment approved and non-priority sector like food processing, service sector, etc. accounts for about 39% of the total investment. This indicates a very high percentage of nearly 40% foreign investment inflows in non-priority sector.

TABLE 6.2

India's Foreign Trade during the Post-Liberalisation Period

(In U.S. $ Million)

Year	*Exports*	*Imports*	*Trade Balance*
1990-91	18145	20073	-5928
1991-92	17866	19411	-1545
	(-1.5)	(-19.4)	
1992-93	18537	21882	-3345
	(3.7)	(12.7)	
1993-94	22173	23212	-1039
	(19.6)	(6.1)	
1993-94 (April-Sept.)	10351	10791	-440
1994-95	11621	12851	-1230
(April-Sept.)	912.3)	(19.1)	

Source: RBI Bulletin, June 1994 and Press release of the Ministry of Commerce, dated November 4, 1994.

The foreign investors have concentrated on two sectors: Power generation and oil extraction, refining and oil products. As stated by Mr. Arun Ghosh, the following facts should be noted in this respect:

(i) with regard to power generation thee is guarantee return of 15%.
(ii) foreign investment in oil sector has been directed only towards proven oil fields.

Global investors are very keen to enter areas which promise quick returns and high profits with short gestation period. This explains the rush and pressures in these areas because the total investment can be repatriated in a period of 1-2 years through high dividends. Secondly, foreign investment is catering to the needs of the upper middle and affluent classes, thus, concentrating on the 180 million consumers. There is an utter neglect of wage goods sector. During 1980-81 to 1992-93 the output of consumer durables increased at an annual average rate of 10% while that of wage goods was as low as 4-5%. Thirdly, 43% of the foreign investment is in the nature of portfolio investment (financial investment) which strengthens speculative trading in shares. The MNCs are rapidly increasing their share holding in Indian companies and are thus swallowing Indian concerns. The process of Indianisation of the corporate sector initiated by Nehru has been totally reserved. This has upset even big industrialists in the private sector and they have organised a protest against these policies under the popularly called—"Bombay Club".

Our moneylenders insisted that we should reduce taxes to the bare minimum and we kept on obliging them. During the last three budgets our losses of revenue due to reduction of taxes were as follows:

TABLE 6.3

Revenue Losses due to Tax Reduction

1993-94	Rs. 11209 crores
1994-95	Rs. 4081 crores
1995-96	Rs. 3292 crores

Source: *Mainstream*, April 8, 1995.

The gap between our tax revenue and revenue expenditure (both non-Plan and Plan) has kept on widening during the last four years. This is explained in the Table 6.4.

Our market borrowing and interest obligation have reached a stage beyond which we should move cautiously. Table 6.5 throws sufficient light on the issue.

We are told that huge foreign direct investment is pouring in but on the ground level we find that MNCs are only engaged in the production of consumer goods for the elite sections of the population. The country requires investment in basic and heavy industry and quick development of rural infrastructure. Employment

Table 6.4

Difference Between Tax Revenue and Revenue Expenditure

(Rs. in crores)

Year	*Revenue Expenditure*	*Tax Revenue*	*Difference*
1992-93	92702	54044	38658
1993-94	108169	53449	54720
1994-95 (Revised)	122902	64988	57914
1995-96 (Budget)	136328	74374	61954

Source: *Business Standard*, March 16, 1995.

opportunities in their project is minimum because their technologies are creating more unemployment in their own country. MNCs are more interested in production of potato chips, soft drinks, cosmetics, boot-polish, detergent power, video games etc. A poor country must step up its capital investment and it is the interest of a developing country to mobilise its savings and depend less on foreign investment. Gross domestic savings as percentage of gross domestic product has declined from 23.7% in 1990-91 to

TABLE 6.5

Borrowing and other Liabilities and Interest Payments

(Rs. in crores)

	1992-93 Actual	*1993-94 Actual*	*1994-95 R.E.*	*1995-96 B.E.*
1. Borrowing and other liabilities	27861	49297	55035	52634
2. Interest	3135	36695	44000	52000
3. Interest as percentage of Non-Plan Expenditure	36	37	39	42

20.2% in 1993-94. The growth rate in gross domestic capital formation at 1980-81 prices was 16% in 1990-91 and has been negative since 1991-92 to 1993-94 varying from (-) 14.2 to (-) 2.4. India must step up its own saving and investment.

The underlying philosophy of the reform measures emphasised macro-economic stabilisation in the short-run and growth in the long-run. The magnitude of the crisis with the fiscal deficits reaching 8.4 per cent of the G.D.P. and the inflation ranging at 17 per cent in 1990-91 certainly called for fire fighting operations. In the first two years the state of government finances seemed to be improving with the fiscal deficit as proportion of G.D.P. coming down from 8.4 per cent in 1990-91 to 5.9 per cent in 1991-92 and 5.7 per cent in 1992-93. This healthy trend could not be maintained and in 1993-94 the fiscal deficits climbed to 7.3 per cent of the G.D.P. However, the slippage seen in 1993-94 has been checked in 1994-95 and fiscal deficit came down from 7.3 per cent to 6 per cent of G.D.P. Such a situation with fiscal management raises the question whether the fiscal changes had really brought about any structural changes in the Central Government's budgetary position. The programme of fiscal compression could not be sustained indefinitely, because all the soft options available to the government to reduce expenditure were already exhausted.

One of the main reasons economists get jittery is that if large budget deficit persists over several years the rate of inflation tends to get out of control. The net effects of all these have been an inflation rate hovering around 10 per cent for most of the last four years.

The cost of globalization even when India is far from integrating with the global economy with its still limited status as a trading nation have begun to bite. It has became evident that the major industrial nations play the rules of game.

On reassessment of the results of the Uruguay Round by the World Bank, the UNCTAD (UN conference on Trade and Development and other international bodies have raised question marks about the degree and spread effects of trade liberalisation of developing countries, especially in agriculture and textiles.

That protectionism and unilateralism still dominate the global scene, has been dramatically highlighted by the dispute between the first two world economies, U.S.A. and Japan over automobiles, which would put the infant W.T.O. to a severe test in its first year.

According to the UNCTAD assessment international competition on prices and quality would intensify as a result of Uruguay Round, leading to the development of new products and processes. In the process there could be potential marginalisation of poor nations and vulnerable Groups within nations. There has been no beginning in lowering the scale of agricultural subsidies in OECD countries and the total support to agriculture in fact increased in 1994.

The developing countries' output now constitutes about 45 per cent of the total world production. The share of manufactures in the total exports of developing countries has increased to 60 per cent from a mere 5 per cent in 1970s. Despite this, the developing countries' share of world trade is only 30 per cent. The developed countries which corner over 7 per cent of the world trade have virtually got their own market saturated. They are now desperately looking out for new markets among the developing countries on the one hand and restrict at the same time access to their own markets on false pleas like social clause and environmental issues.

EXPERIENCE OF OTHER COUNTRIES

A year ago a major World Bank Report, surveying Latin America reforms proclaimed "The consultants and academics are analysing the Chilean and Mexican experience to learn first hand, how these countries which only a few years ago seemed hopeless are becoming increasingly attractive to the international business. The reform process in Mexico is mature and appears consolidated." The same consultants and academicians are indeed once again examining the Mexican experience as Mexico drops into a deep recession.

The structural reforms in the Mexican economy began in the mid-eighties. By the early 90s its success in deregulation and liberalisation particularly in liberalising trade regime and reducing government deficits were widely praised. The pendulum began to swing in early 1994. High interest rates and open capital account led to attract large capital inflows underpinning on overvalued peso and fueling a growing current account deficits which reached 8% of GDP in 1994.

The history of international lending over the last century is replete with boom and bust cycles of depressing regularity. The revolution in finance, driven by rapid changes in information technologies and in financial instruments has made international financial market much more volatile than in the past.

The economic crisis in Mexico is being widely discussed in terms of its implications for India, Political instability, corruption, growing inequality and austerity measures as debt rescue efforts causing hardship to the people are some of the causes of the crisis. The Mexican debt was estimated at 80 billion dollars in 1982. The debt rescue efforts involved an austerity programme of the IMF-led cut in subsidies making the life hard for the common masses. As much as 12 billion dollars a year was being paid for debt service.

The President of the Inter-American Development Bank himself a Mexican estimated that capital flight from Mexico during 1979-83 amounted to about 90 billion dollars more than the total debt of 80 dollars.

It has been estimated that just 35 of Mexico's richest

families grabs a higher share of income than the poorest 15 million. This is the amazing extent of inequalities in Mexico. These coupled with rising inflation aggravated the problem. The lesson for us is that without removing such basic distortions, any attempt to solve the country's economic problems simply by inviting foreign investment and opening up the economy is not going to help us.

A massive study by Michaely reveals that a wide variety of trade and economic liberalisation which started before or after oil-shock were reversed by 1993. Success in South Korea and Taiwan is not related as much to the role of free enterprise and the market as to state intervention. Their governments protected industries and subsidized exports. South Korea industrial development strategy was guided by the Economic Planning Board. Six industries—steel, metal machine building, ship building, electronics and chemicals were targeted for intense government support and development, despite stiff opposition from the IMF and the World Bank.

There is of course another side of the East Asian miracle industrial growth, accentuated income inequality intensified class conflict, underlined agriculture and degraded environment. In Korea and Taiwan, the benefits of land reforms of the 1950s were reversed in the 1970s when resources from agriculture were squeezed to build up industries for exports. Even after 25 years of industrial growth, these economies remain crucially dependent on Japan. In Korea, for example, 90 per cent of machines are still imported from Japan. In Indonesia and Malaysia industrial growth has increased economic disparities and thereby generated intense class conflicts. The foreign advisors in these countries now advocate growth first, democracy later.

No great industrialist is going to come and look after the primary health centres. No multinational is going to run the primary school. However, well the market forces allocate resources, they do not respond to common needs. Common needs for sustainable development, education, health and social security can only be articulated and met by people and their government.

AN OBJECTIVE EVALUATION OF NEP

The entire exercise of New Economic Policy has initiated a process of jobless growth. The silent implementation of exit policy has led to voluntary retirement on a massive scale. In the name of reducing cost and making enterprise more competitive private sector enterprises have engaged experts for reducing the workforce. In TISCO, the management is working on a plan to reduce its workforce from about seven thousand to 3 to 4 thousand. The fear of losing jobs have made the officers and the workers restless. The Government as the protector of the interest of the employees has left the scene. This prevailing sense of helplessness and insecurity in the minds of the workforce exposes the ugly face of the NEP. The New Economic Policy has also led to casualisation of labour which enjoyed better social securities earlier. The capital intensive path of development has resulted into jobless growth. Sudipto Mundle of the National Institute of Public Finance has concluded with the help of a study that the stabilisation programme raised unemployment rate from less than 4 per cent in 1991-92 to 5 per cent in 1992-93.

The major causes of inefficiency in public sector units have been bureaucratisation, political interference in decision-making, deterioration in work ethics, etc. The concepts of M.O.U., workers equity participation and disinvestment of P.S.U.'s equity have been put to practice to reduce losses. It is argued that loss-making P.S.U.s be privatised. In practice, it is the healthy and high profit sector undertakings whose shares are being offered for investment.

The three international organisations—World Bank, IMF and WTO are supposed to serve the interests of only the G-7 countries. On the pressure of these countries we are ordered to dismantle our public sector undertakings and reduce import duties, excise duties and direct taxes. The external constraints on national development remained manageable in India until 1965. But following the Government's failure in implementing land reforms and making the economy self-reliant and the emergence of the crisis in the global system, the external pressure became formidable. The process of development was significantly influenced by foreign interests. It moved counter to local factor endowment and disregarded the requirements of our population.

It is debatable whether any package of reform which focused solely on a long-term objective of promoting growth can be sustainable in the country. This was clearly recognised by the government. Thus, although the fiscal compression programme in a cut in the size of the poverty alleviation and rural development programmes and more generally in social sector spending in the first couple of years, this trend was reserved dramatically in the last two budgets. There has been increased allocation for J.R.Y., elementary education and health care.

Since no data on income or consumption distribution are available beyond 1992, it is possible to come to any definite conclusion about the impact of the reform process on the poor. However, increasing concerns have been expressed about "reforms with a human race". The process of structural adjustment initiated in India in 1991 is far from complete. The pace of reforms have been very slow. It has failed to achieve even the short-term goal of restoring fiscal stability.

CONCLUSION

We must never forget that the fundamental objective of economic reforms and indeed of all economic policies of the Government should be to bring about a sustained improvement in the living standard of the people of India, especially of the poor. Rapid and sustained growth of output and employment opportunities is the surest antidote to our daunting problem of poverty. An important factor determining the quality of life of India's people, is the quality of public goods and services provided by all levels of government. This includes police, legal education, health, etc.

If we try to judge the performance of the reform package in terms of the objectives stated above, it can be easily concluded that it is not encouraging. It has neither liberated the economy from the clutches of the bureaucratic and political controls nor has integrated it globally. The steps taken for restoration of macro-economic stability and revival of growth in output and employment, have failed to yield sufficient results. The fiscal deficit continues to be high. There is continuing inflationary pressure. These have made the life of the poor miserable and hard. Whether little growth has taken place is jobless. Now the people talk of "market plus" and "reform with human face".

The Brettons Woods Institutions must be made transparent. Their policies and programmes should be made people centered. Global macro-economic policy should address the structure of poverty and stimulate the level of real purchasing power. It will to look into the distribution of income and wealth both between and within countries leading to a democratisation of consumption. Global production and consumption must stay within the limits of carrying capacity of the earth.

Structural adjustment programmes have negative effect on social development goals such as eradication of poverty, promotion of employment and social integration. Multilateral development banks and donors should complement adjustment lending with enhanced targeted social development investment lending. The reality of an imperfection must be recognised. Social development, which is directly linked with the improvement in the quality of human life is not subordinate to economic growth. It is a core issue and not a marginal one.

It becomes rather imperative to intervene in markets to prevent or counteract market failure and to harmonise economic and social development including the development and implementation of appropriate programmes that would entitle and enable people living in poverty and disadvantage to participate fully and productive in the economy and society. There is an urgent need for analysis and continuous review of the macro-economic, micro-economic and sectorial policies and their impact on poverty, employment, social integration and social development.

The Copenhagen Declaration has urged rich nations to spend 0.7 per cent of their GNP on foreign aid and cancel debt of poor countries. The donor countries should earmark 20 per cent of their budgets on similar programmes.

A research study of the World Bank of about 8 high performing Asian economies concludes that their superior record of growth is largely due to superior accumulation of physical and human capital. The task of the government is to raise the productivity of investment both in private and public sector, Everything cannot be handled effectively either by private sector or by public sector. We have failed to emphasise the productivity of investment and for that public sector has failed in India and if we overlook this productivity aspect of both physical and human capital, the private sector also is not going to succeed. Arrangement for health, education, infrastructure, etc. should be the responsibility of state, since market mechanism cannot deliver good. Nehruvian model of mixed economy with a bit opening is more relevant today as ever before. Joan Robinson has rightly said that the invisible hand can work by strangulation.

We are critical of the lack of commitment on the

part of the North to reach the promised 0.7 per cent of GNP as aid, at the same time it is to be noted that something like Rs. 50,000 crores of foreign aid remain unutilised by India. Instead of criticising others for not giving us more, we should ask ourselves some question on what we are doing with what we have got. It is now difficult for India to go back to the old track but it does not mean that it should not move with caution, confidence and self-respect towards building a self-reliant vibrant and strong economy.

India's global linkages at the commercial level have though improved, the technology and finance are yet to flow from India to other parts of the world, so that the country can capitalise on its emerging global commercial relationship at bilateral as well as group level. It should also try to gain membership of one or more economic block or grouping, strengthening bilateral relations with countries who have access to the markets of such large groupings. New opportunities have been opened. The proper utilisation of these opportunities may lead India's transition from an aid seeking, poorly developed and overpopulated nation to an industrially modern and an egalitarian society where quality of life would make every Indian proud.

While addressing the Copenhagen World Summit for Social Development (March 6-12, 1995) Shri Chhedi Jagan rightly stated that there was necessity for a new global human order in which the needs, hopes and aspiration of each citizen would assume primary importance in the era of jobless growth, jobless recovery and massive social injustice in both the North and the South. In the same summit it was accepted by the Indian Prime Minister Shri P.V. Narasimha Rao that one could not help the uneasy feeling that what is needed really is a certain market plus, otherwise the poor and the weak are likely to suffer exclusion due to the imperfections of the market.

The world capitalism has now entered into a critical phase. In a recently published book, 'Age of Extremes', its writer Eric Hobsbawn sees capitalism as a restless and insatiable social, economic and cultural system which relaxes only when, there is nothing left unconquered. It does not proceed smoothly. It begins with crisis and ends with crisis. He further argues that the present economic scene is dominated by three major structural transformation. The first is the end of Eurocentricity because of internationalism of capitalism. The second is the emergence of the globe as a single operational unit. The third is the transformation in the pattern of human relationships. The collapse of much or rural society together with increasing privatistion of life in the First World has disrupted the pattern of the traditional social relationships. He concludes.

"Age of extreme ends in 1991 with capitalism now largely uncontrolled and with its real world alternatives either destroyed or discarded. A system that places growth above all other goals creates incentives for capital to externalise social and environmental costs, generate jobless growth, derogates the rights of workers and undermines the role of the trade unions."

7

*Foreign Investment and India's Fragile Economy**

OM PRAKASH*

I am beholden to Osmania University (Hyderabad) and the Indian Commerce Association for inviting me to deliver this Memorial Lecture in honour of an industrial luminary so brilliant as Sir Padampat Singhania who captained the Indian Commerce Association as its first President, and who sat in the front row of Indian businessmen for as long as half a century. Having come into personal contact with this great leader of Industry and Commerce, I am happy to reminisce the celebrated Seminar on Business Leadership in India which I had occasion to convene as the Professor-Director of the School of Commerce, University of Rajasthan, Jaipur in February 1968. It was the most prestigious event organised as part of the Twentieth Anniversary Celebrations of our University. The Seminar had been inaugurated by Seth G.D. Birla, the doyen of Indian industry, while the great Sir Padampat was to deliver the Valedictory Address in the afternoon of the concluding

* The present paper is the full text of the lecture delivered by Prof. Om Prakash in the memory of Sir Padampat Singhania.

day. It was during the lunch hour that I went to see him. I thought that it might be difficult to contact him at the odd hour. But, to my pleasant surprise, he was in harness, having donned *Churidar Pyjama*, with *Sherwani* just waiting to be put on; as such, he was quite "ready for the event". That, in fact, was the practical philosophy of his life *all along*.

Padampat, known as "Mitthoo Baboo" in his childhood, was born on the 3rd of February, 1905. Incidentally, his birth closely followed that of J.R.D. Tata (in 1904) who held the banner of India high in the industrial world. This corroborates the view that superb achievers in a field, be it that of Commerce, Science or Art, come to this world in clusters, so that, while there is a galaxy of contemporaries during the era, there are other periods of virtual vacuum marked by mediocrity *sans* any recognised leaders. Some two hundred years back, Sir Padampat Singhania's ancestors had migrated from Rajasthan to Kanpur *via* Farrukhabad in U.P. Their business was run under the name of Baijnath Ramnath, funding cotton mills in Kanpur during the second half of the 19th century, and early part of 20th century. Padampat's father, Lala Kamlapat Singhania, founded the Juggilal Kamlapat Cotton Mills in 1920, thus ushering in the-now-famous buzzword "J.K." in the business world. He was the first Indian to set up a cotton mill in Kanpur. However, L. Kamlapat's life span (1884-1937) was rather short (just 53). At the time of his father's death. Padampat was only 32 but, as the eldest son, he assumed leadership of the J.K. Group. Both he and the Group attained astounding progress during the next 42 years that he lived. His end came on November 18, 1979, with a longevity of 74, twenty-one years old than that of his father, but fifteen years less than that of J.R.D. Tata, who died at the ripe old age of 89 in 1993. After being knighted in 1943, Sir Padampat Singhania had come to be called as "Sir Sahib" instead of "Padampatji".

Some institutions, particularly in the domain of

education and medicine, which bear the imprint of Sir Padampat Singhania's charitable and humanistic character, include the J.K. Institute of Applied Physics (with a renowned scientist like.Krishnaji having been it's Professor Director) at the University of Allahabad. Inaugurated on the 4th of January, 1949, the Institute was dedicated to the nation by the Prime Minister, Pandit Jawaharlal Nehru, in 1956. The subject of Physics at Allahabad had been nurtured by such stalwarts as Dr. M.N. Saha (who had migrated from Calcutta) and Sir K.S. Krishnan, the co-author of "Raman Krishnan Effect", later known as simply "Raman Effect", after the Nobel Prize had been given to Sir C.V. Raman (whose name was associated with the Institute at Bangalore). Sir K.S. Krishnan had just moved to Delhi as the first Chief of the National Physical Laboratory. As such, Sir Padampat's choice of donation in favour of the University of Allahabad was based on the acid academic test. "Consideration of kinship in the matter of work never weighted with him. It was hard work and efficiency alone which attracted his attention". This is the testimony from Mr. Sohanlal Singhania (Senior Director, J.K. Organisation, and In-charge of Rajasthan enterprises, specially in Kota) who died only recently after being Sir Padampat's close contemporary for half a century. The University of Lucknow, too, was an early beneficiary of Sir Padampat's philanthropy manifested in the J.K. Institute of Sociology and Human Relations. This institute flourished under the academic leadership of Dr. Radhakamal Mookerjee, one of the two economic theorists of India quoted in international classics like "Economics of Welfare" (where Professor A.C. Pigou quoted Dr. Mookerjee) and "Economics of Imperfect Competition" (where Mrs. Joan Robinson quoted Professor J.K. Mehta of the University of Allahabad). Soon after Sir Padampat's death, the JAYKAYLON Mother and Child Health Institute was inaugurated at Jaipur by the Governor of Rajasthan, Mr. Raghukul Tilak, on the 26th of January, 1980, when Dr. P.K. Sethi (winner of Guinners Award for his "Jaipur Foot", and decorated with Ramon Magsaysay Award in

1981) was the Principal of Sawai Man Singh (SMS) Medical College.

Like some other big industrialists of his time Sir Padampat Singhania was not inducted into much of formal education, much less into any Institute of Business Management or Department of Economics. But his common sense was sturdy, and his interest in high/ professional education was abiding. He had his hand in the establishment of the Indian Institute of Technology at Kanpur, an institution which he nursed as Chairman of the Board of Governors for no less than seven years (1965-72). As visiting Professor at Kanpur University during 1991-92 for their newly started MBA Programme run by the Institute of Business Management, I found the IIT (Kanpur) Library the best in the country. Sir Padampat also founded the Merchants Chamber of U.P., and occupied the coveted position of the President of FICCI (Federation of the Indian Chambers of Commerce and Industry) in 1935 at the young age of 30. On the 21st of December 1946, he presented his credentials as a Member of the Constituent Assembly of India, and took oath as a member of provisional Parliament on the 22nd of February, 1950. Sir Padampat's observations won appreciation from outstanding Parliamentarians like Dr. Shyama Prasad Mookerjee (then Minister for Industry in the Central Cabinet). It is unfortunate that Sir Padampat's indepth comments on Devaluation and Foreign Investment were not heeded to by many of the Finance Ministers (with the notable exception of Sir C.D. Deshmukh) and other powers-that-be in the Government of India. Here are some relevant quotations.

On Devaluation (6th of October, 1949)

"Money does not barter with money. It is material that barters with material. Instead of going into a detailed explanation, what I suggest, our Government ought to do is this. Before the devaluation came about, in the world market, supposing Indian jute, or other Indian raw material or Indian product in terms of payment bought a certain amount of iron, steel or manufactured goods from outside, the Ministry should index that figure. They should see that our raw material does not buy any less than what it was buying before the devaluation. They should see that no harm is done to the country as a whole. . . For the sake of example let me say that for one machine which I have to import I used to pay, in terms of raw materials, 10 maunds of jute. If tomorrow as a result of the devaluation I have to pay for the same machine by sending 15 maunds of jute then there is poverty in the country".

On Foreign Investment (Dollar Loan—6th of October, 1949)

"For the rehabilitation of the country it is necessary that we should get loans from foreign countries, but I would request the Honorable Finance Minister and the Cabinet as a whole that they should examine this problem from this point of view. What does the dollar loan mean to us today? The dollar loan which we have received upto now, if we have to pay it back in dollars after rehabilitation, would become from 30 million dollars to 40 millions in terms of our country. The rate of interest at 3 per cent plus 1.5 per cent commission amounts to 4.5 per cent and free of income tax means a total of 8.5 per cent. If you are going to incur an economic loss to the country, are you going into economic subjection and remain always a gulam (slave) to the foreign loan?"

FOREIGN INVESTMENT (1991-96)

Now that we have seen five complete years of the so-called liberalisation of the Indian economy, it may be pertinent to look at the sector-wise break-up of Foreign Direct Investment (FDI) represented by foreign collaboration approvals between the 1st of August, 1991, and the 31st of July, 1996, as noted below:

S. No.	*Sector*	*Number of Collaborations*	*Amount Approved (Rs. Crore)*
1.	Telecommunications	266	19488
2.	Fuel (Power and Oil Refineries)	229	16681
3.	Service Sector	320	5208
4.	Transportation Industry	447	5129
5.	Food Processing Industry	512	5122
6.	Metallurgical Industry	351	4993
7.	Chemicals (other than Fertilizers)	957	4758
8.	Electrical Engineering	1559	4218
9.	Hotels and Tourism	171	1947
10.	Textiles	318	1625
11.	Miscellaneous Industries	3887	8966

N.B. Total (Technical Plus Financial) Number of Approvals.

Thus the total FDI approved during these five years aggregated to Rs. 78135 crore. However, the actual inflow was estimated to be less than 20 per cent (one fifth) of this figure, i.e. of the order of Rs. 15000 crore only. The amounts to just about two per cent of the total investment envisaged under the Eighth Five-Year Plan, i.e., of the order of Rs. 800000 crore. Actual FDI inflow peaked at Rs. 6369 crore for the calendar year 1995, when (as on December 31, 1995) the aggregate (actual) inflow (since August 1991) stood at Rs. 12154 crore. That is, the actual inflow during 1995 was more than the entire inflow between August 1, 1991 and December 31, 1994 (three years and five months). Actual inflow during 1994 stood at Rs. 2971 crore, a substantial improvement over Rs. 1786 crore for 1993, Rs. 675 crore for 1992 and Rs. 351 crore for 1991.

Analysing the amounts approved under FDI, it would appear that about half fell in the crore sector, roughly one-fourth in the consumer sector, and the remaining one-fourth in what may be called as the twilight zone. In other words, only half of the total approvals could be deemed to be really relevant for India's basic growth. A further dissection of the core sector reveals that FDI approved in respect of Fuel (Power and Oil Refineries), amounting to about one-half of the approvals in this sector (or, one-fourth of the total approvals), had remained practically unfructified. During the debate on the confidence motion (May 1996) presented by Prime Minister Atal Behari Vajpayee, it was pointed out on the floor of the Lok Sabha (and, as such, may be taken as a full truth, even though a bitter one) that not a single MW of power had been added during the era of economic liberalisation (a result of foreign investment). Gestation period is the usual alibi. But, obviously, it is not just "economic" or "technical gestation"; there is lot of "legal gestation", along with "political gestation", as in the case of ENRON's Dabhol Power Project in Maharashtra. Although the Mumbai High Court dismissed the writ petitions against the Central and State Government agencies on the 2nd of December, 1996, it is doubtful if the project work can really restart soon in view of the likely appeal before the Supreme Court. So far as self-sufficiency in oil is concerned, we have actually moved in the back gear during the year of economic liberalisation which has just completed five years (1991-96). Domestic production is now meeting a much smaller part of the domestic demand, so that the imports dependence ratio has gone up in an alarming manner. During the first seven months (April-October 1996) of the current accounting year (1996-97), the oil bill shot up by 43 per cent to $ 5.2 billion, as against $ 3.6 billion for the corresponding months of the previous year. In contrast to this, the growth in India's total exports was less than 10 per cent during this period. Oil imports consumed as much as 28 per cent of India's total export earnings.

TELECOM is the only sector which has manifested some quick movements of a core character. But these stand overshadowed by serious allegations (1996) of high level corruption (Rs. 1200 crore) which is being looked into by courts and other authorities. There is also the dark side of supersonic developments in sophisticated technology. Cellular phones, the pager, the internet and the like tend to diminish the human peace of mind, and add to the exiting bundle of tensions. Not only that, these techniques to go widen the gulf between the rich and the poor, between the privileged and the disprivileged, as also between the powerful and the powerless, thus heightening social tensions, frustration and conflict. The same is the outcome of foreign investment in ostentatious consumer goods industries, specially food processing. For example, when a packet containing just fifty grams of potato chips is sold for fifteen rupees (giving a per kilogram rate of three hundred—or at least two hundred, with liberal allowance for packing cost—rupees) poor parents of children find themselves in great agony and much embarrassment. Staggering 16 per cent of the rural population of India have access to less than three rupee a day, which is less than the cost of (one kilogram of) potatoes. Another 18 per cent though slightly better, with five rupees a day, find themselves in the same boat with the current Jaipur cost (six rupees per kilogram as on December 4, 1996) of potatoes. These are the findings of the National Council of Applied Economic Research (Principle Economist, Dr. Abusalef Shariff) in a report appearing in the daily press on this date.

Route-wise, direct investment has been classified into three categories. The first one is RBI's automatic route which figured at zero in 1991-92, and remained relatively insignificant during subsequent years. The SIA/FIPB route (second one) has accounted for roughly half of the FDI since 1991-92. NRIs, constituting the third route, have contributed about one-third of FDI inflow over several years. However, NRI inflows are subject to a great deal of volatility; and, rates of interest and other conditions applicable to such inflows have been changed time and again to prevent sudden/substantial outflows or to buttress the inflow process. Besides direct investment, there is portfolio investment which, again has a three fold classification. Foreign Institutional Investors (FIIs) representing the first category, stood at zero in 1991-92 and at a negligible future in 1992-93.

Thereafter, they claimed close to half of the portfolio investment. The other important category of Euro-Equities, which also had stood at zero in 1991-92, was able to improve its contribution to roughly half by 1994-95. Offshore funds and others, representing the third category, remained at insignificant levels during 1991-92 and 1992-93; the same had risen to about ten per cent of portfolio investment in 1993-94 followed by vicissitudes thereafter.

While addressing the special session of India-Canada Joint Business Council (NBC) organised by FICCI and ASSOCHAM in January 1996, the RBI Governor, Dr. C. Rangarajan, revealed that total inflow of foreign investment (including both direct and portfolios investment) had risen from a mere $ 154 million in 1991-92 to $ 4895 million in 1994-95. For the first eight months (April-November 1995) of the financial year 1995-96, he placed the figure markedly lower at $ 2.2 billion ($4.1 billion for full year, 1995-96). Accordingly to him, FIIs from 19 countries had invested in fairly diversified industries, while also participating in public sector disinvestments. But here lies the rub. Allowing foreign investors to acquire control, even though partial, over India's public enterprises may be a dangerous proposition. The recent (October 1996) issue of Global Depository Receipts (GDRs) by the State Bank of India, a Public Corporation created under an Act of Parliament in 1995, is a case in point. This institution was meant to serve agriculture and the rural folk in particular. If at all, shares should have been issued to poor farmers to give them a sense of ownership over this national institution. Even if the foreign investors are able to muster four of the 32 Directorships, there may be detrimental deviation in SBI's policy decisions and outlook. Again, with an already high capital adequacy ratio of 11-12 per cent as against the prescribed minimum of eight per cent, there was no case at all to approach the capital market, and much less to appease the foreign investors.

INDIA'S FRAGILE ECONOMY

Whether we view the domestic domain, or examine the external equilibrium, Indian economy has been fragile all along during the last five years of economic liberalisation (1991-96). Let us move our first foot on the foreign front, since that has been claimed to be most formidable, with phenomenal focus on foreign exchange reserves. According to "*Economic Survey 1995-96: An Update*", there was an increase foreign currency reserves from $ 2.2 billion in March 1991 to over $ 20 billion in March 1995 which, however, declined to $ 17 billion in March 1966. These do not include Gold and SDRs which, if taken into account, woula dwarf the degree of increase from $ 5.8 billion in March 1991 to a little over $ 25 billion in March 1995 and about $ 22 billion in March 1996. However, it needs to be noted that the value of gold had been raised several-fold through a book entry in the wake of the 1990-91 foreign exchange crisis. Regarding reserves "other than Gold and SDRs", the crucial question to be answered is: "What proportion of these reserves, if any, is earnings-based". The honest answer would be: "Nil"; for, in none of the last five financial years between 1st April 1991 and 31st March 1996, have been able to see my favourable balance of trade. Are we not throwing dust into the eyes of lay persons when we pass others' money as our own? Do we not know that borrowings from IMF, World Bank and other official/non-official lenders have to be, some day, repaid and with interest? Are we unaware of the fact that any NRI inflow creates a countervailing liability for NRI outflow along with hefty interest burden worked out at a preferential rate phenomenally different from the one applicable to domestic deposits? Do we deny that even equity participation under FDI/JV arrangements can be withdrawn when it so pleases the foreign investors? Should we be obvious of the propensity of FIIs (capable of buying out the entire capitalization of our Stock Exchanges) to destabilise the external value of the Indian rupee and to aggravate our foreign exchange disequilibrium?

At this point, it would be relevant to recount what Sir Padampat Singhania deposed on the 6th of October 1949, before the Constituent Assembly with regard to Devaluation and Foreign Investment, as quoted under (under para 2 and 3 of page 4) in the first section of this Lecture. The global movement toward liberalisation may be said to have set in around 1980 when the basic exchange rate of the U.S. Dollar in terms of Indian Rupee was Rs. 7.86. I had gone up to Rs. 21.14 by the 28th June, 1991. The immediate impact of India's liberalisation programme was to push up this rate to Rs. 25.95 by the 3rd of July 1991. The RBI reference rate on the 3rd of December, 1996, was Rs. 35.70 (with occasional bumps well beyond this during the intervening period). The devaluation of 1949, had raised the cost of a dollar from "three rupees and five annas" to four rupees and twelve annas". For some fourteen years following the 1966 devaluation, the exchange rate had remained fairly stable around Rs. 7.50 for a dollar. The U.S. Dollar now (3rd December 1996) is more than ten times costlier than what obtained before the 1949 devaluation; about five times the rate prevailing during 1966-80; and roughly 70 per cent more than the rate recorded on the 28th of June, 1991. To use Sir Padampat's language, we have now to export 17 tonnes of iron ore (whose price remains controlled under long-term agreement), instead of ten tonnes (prior of July 1991) to earn the same amount of foreign exchange in terms of dollars. If accounting is done in Japanese currency, we would need to export more than 20 tonnes of iron ore instead of 10 tonnes, since the cost of yen went up from 15.31 paise on the 28th of June 1991, to 30.90 paise on the 3rd of December, 1966. On the other hand, for importing machinery or motor car costing $ 10,000 from the U.S.A., we would now need a sum of roughly Rs. 3,60,000 as against some thing like Rs. 2,10,000 before July 1991 (ignoring the price increase in America during the intervening period). If the price of that machinery or motor car in the U.S.A. stood at around $ 5,000 at the earlier date, the rupee requirement would appear to have increased by about "three times and a half" (from a little over one lakh of rupees to roughly Rs. 3,60,000). Thus, whether we call it devaluation, depreciation or exchange rate adjustment, thus fruits of liberalisation have been bitter. They clearly indicate the degree of deterioration in India's competitive position (particularly in relation to the developed world), some thing which the process of liberalisation was designed to strengthen in the global context. So to pay, we are permitting abject national exploitation under the euphoria of economic jargons and high sounding slogans.

On the domestic front, inability to control fiscal deficits has actually *fractured* the Indian economy (far beyond the stage of *fragility*). The banner of liberalisation was raised with the (implicit) assumption that Governments tend to be inefficient and corrupt; hence they should be cut to size. For the year 1993, a target of reduction to other tune of 10,000 jobs was laid; but, actually, there was an expansion to the extent of 40,000 posts in the Government of India, as revealed in a study conducted by the Confederation of Indian Industry (CII). During the year 1995-96, the Central Government is reported to have fattened by some 70,000 new positions. Chapter 7, entitled "Toward Better and Slimmer Government", of *World Development Report 1966* reads": "The transaction from plan to market calls for a wholesale reinvention of government. The state has to move from doing many things badly to doing its fewer core tasks well. This means government must at once shrink and change its nature".

If this is not done, the consumption expenditure of the Government would continue to cause huge revenue deficits, more so after the likely implementation of new pay scales in 1997. Thus, more of capital receipts (borrowed at 15 per cent rate of interest or so) would be eaten up, leaving still less for investment/development. This would further fan the fire of inflation which would, besides aggravating the hardship of poor persons, seriously undermine India's competitive position in export markets. Finally this would impinge on the levels of production, productivity, growth, employment and overall welfare of the people.

Another matter of serious concern for India's domestic economy is the neglect of agriculture and the rural sector. Foodgrain production has suffered a setback from 191.1 million tonnes in 1994-95 to 190.4 million tonnes (preliminary estimate) in 1995-96. Just in about a month's time (between October-November 1996) retail prices of wheat have soared from Rs. 7.50 to Rs. 10 per Kg. in Jaipur's retail markets. Even the Public Distribution System (PDS) has failed to gear up. The hollow announcement on August 15, 1995 for providing mid-day meals to eleven core children cannot be fulfilled; it needs Rs. 4,00,000 crore to be meaningful. The Interim Budget February 1996) had visualised a revenue of Rs. 1,27,000 crore for 1996-97, out of which there was a committed burden of interest to the tune of Rs. 60,000 crore. If a provision of Rs. 40,000 crore is made for midday meals, and the defence budget is managed within the remaining sum of Rs. 27,000 crore, nothing would be left for any other time of expenditure (including salaries, etc. of Government servants). For 1992 according to the NSS method, Rural Poverty, was estimated at 41.7 per cent while Urban Poverty was placed at 37.8 per cent. The number of rural poor (2690 lakhs) was more than thrice the number of urban poor (858 lakhs). These figures came to light in August 1995. Suddenly, in the beginning of January 1996, half baked statistics (preliminary, based on half the sample) were brought forward for 1993, indicating that only 21.68 per cent of rural population and 11.55 per cent of urban population (18.96 per cent of total population) stood below the poverty line. Poverty alleviation cannot be achieved by such miraculous manipulation. That some 40 per cent of the rural population lives below the poverty line is well confirmed by a very careful survey conducted by the National Council of Applied Economic Research, the results appearing in the press on December 4, 1996.

In fine, I may make the following suggestions regarding Foreign investment and India's Fragile Economy:

(1) A completely open door policy regarding foreign investment is economically unsound and psychologically self-defeating. The policy should be linked with access to core technology.

(2) Greater reliance should be placed on domestic savings along with restoration and enhancement of tax incentives.

(3) The policy of running the Government on the basis of TDS (tax deducted at source, the excess of which is not refunded for years together) should be given up.

(4) Instead of trying to maximize revenue, Government should try to minimise (consumption) expenditure. Income tax Department should concentrate attention on a small number of rich assessees, instead of trying to scatter efforts by roping in many people with modest means.

(5) Mergers, takeovers, and other arrangements likely to restrict competition or promote monopoly, whether initiated by multinational corporations (MNCs) or domestic business leaders, should be promptly checkmated.

(6) Before approving a foreign investment proposal, the likely liability in respect of outflow on account of interest, dividend, repatriation (in dollar terms or other foreign currency) should be suitably weighted in balance.

(7) The concept of level playing field should imply that domestic enterprise (whether private or public) should not be denied any facility (such as 16 per cent guaranteed return) which is made available to foreign investors.

(8) National Institutions like LIC and GIC, which have stood the test of time, smeet M Singhania (grandson of Sir Padampat Singhania staying

in Delhi) at Jaipur in September 1996. I am grateful to him and to Mr. K.V. Murthy, (Asstt. Vice-President, J.K. Cement Works, Kanpur) for supplying me with valuable information regarding Sir Padampat.

References

I happened to meet Mr. Ramapat Singhania (gradson of Sir Padampat Singhania staying in Delhi) at Jaipur in September 1996. I am grateful to him and to Mr. K.V. Murty, (Asstt. Vice-President , J.K. Cement Works, Kanpur) fop supplying me with valuable information regarding Sir Padampat.

J.K. Review, Vol. XXXXI, No. 1, March 1980, p. 10.

Ibid., p. 11.

The Economic Times, New Delhi, September 20, 1996.

Ibid., December 3, 1996.

The Hindustan Times, New Delhi, December 4, 1996.

Economic Survey, 1995-96: An Update, *Government of India*, Ministry of Finance, Economic Division, New Delhi, July 1996, p. 3.

From Plan to Market, World Development Report, 1996, *Oxford University Press/World Bank*, Washington, D.C. (June 27, 1996), p. 110.

The National Council of Applied Economic Research (New Delhi), after four years of study of 33,000 rural households in 16 States, looking in 300 parameters, has come out with a human development profile of rural India that should shudder down the spins of development authorities and the affluent who are putting down hard cash for their second Cielo, their third BPL television etc. or the latest micro oven. The 1994 report, released in Bhopal on the 30th of November, 1996, at a Government of Madhya Pradesh/UNDP workshop, reveals that 39 per cent of the rural population is living below the poverty line Cf. *The Hindustan Times, op. cit.*, front page.

8

*Industrial Finance and Banking in India: A Changing Profile**

D.S. Ganguly

The massive investments in the public sector has brought—in its wake a structural change in the profile of industrial finance. The domain of industry under the ownership and management of private investors in the past found initial finance in the form of equity capital principally from the private investors and the working capital from the bankers and there was no institution for development finance, and the span and limitation of ventures can well be discerned under the circumstances. But in the context of Industrial Policy Resolution, 1956, a patent change become evident due to the wisdom of the government to irrigate the respective domains of the public sector and the private sector through the creation and operation of development financial institutions whose principal role being pronounced as supplier of

* Excerpts from Professor S.K. Basu Memorial Lecture delivered by Dr. D.S. Ganguly, Former Professor and Head, Department of Commerce, Burdwan University, West Bengal, at XLII, All India Commerce Conference held at BIT, MESRA, Ranchi.

development finance to the industrial establishment not only providing the starter but also financing the schemes of expansion of the establishments and this tended to inject spirit of venturism in the entrepreneurs.

The Policy of the Government is to ensure growth of the critical areas of economic sector with appropriate priority determination. This objective can be largely achieved and fulfilled provided the dominant agencies and providers of finance can be brought under the ownership and directional control of the state. This thought was translated into action by invoking the policy of nationalisation of the commercial banks in order to ensure for the state to control the "commanding heights of economy" (14 banks were nationalised in July, 1969 and 6 banks in April, 1980). This nationalisation is a conscious switch-over to accelerate the banking sector into activity in unchartered areas concomitant with the desideratum of new economy to be evenly balanced, bringing forth a new social milieu of distributive justice which entails shedding the dead-weight of conservatism and adoption of aggressive dynamism in operations and providing credit to the priority sector. Though a host of other financing institutions, principally, Life Insurance Corporation of India (LIC), General Insurance Corporation of India (GIC), Unit Trust of India (UTI) and a few private investment and financing houses with their built-in finance are operating, commercial banks still hold the reins of the chariot. The growth and expansion of commercial banking sector in India are, indeed, too patent to ignore.

There has been significant change in the commercial banking sector after 1970 following the momentum of nationalisation pressed into this sector both in the dimension of expansion and character of bank credit. The changes are, however the outcome of changes in macro-economic policies formulated very consciously by the government in which the national economic development was conceived as charged with ideology of egalitarian society and the commercial banks were to assume a locomotive role in speed up ahead. The active support as evident from the side of the government and the over-bearing restrictive policy of Reserve Bank of India (RBI) was mellowed down to a considerable extent towards liberalisation of bank credit with emphasis on advances to the priority sector and expansion in rural and backward regions even at the risk of narrowing down the profitability and liquidity position of banks to a great extent with a caution sounded, however, by the Central Bank against over-doings by commercial banks that may cause destabilisation of economy. In fact, Reserve Bank of India, as the Central Bank of the country cannot afford to loosen the strings of control over money market and in this a perfect harmony between the thinkings of the Planning Commission and Reserve Bank of India is conducive. Happily, in the development planning concept and modalities the macro-economic policies India framed far in symbolise the harmonious thinking in tandem between the government, the Planning Commission and the Central Bank in the effort of ensuring economic growth with stability and social justice.

DEVELOPMENT BANKING

Development banking is a recent thinking and the different non-bank financial institutions have been established with specific purpose of supplying development finance to the public sector as well as the private sector. The restrictions imposed on commercial banks in respect of term-loan buttresses the need of financial agencies which may meet the needs of long-term industrial finance. Development finance does not only connote initial finance needed for establishing an industry or project in which capital goods involve the dominant portion of finance for infrastructure and machinery and plant together with the cost of installation and building the township appropriate to the industry in a particular environment but also finance for future expansion of the projects. Development banking has to be, of course, geared to the macro-economic policies of the government which lay down *inter alia* the contours of industrial entrepreneurship to be accorded acceptability in the context of socio-economic periphery envisaged by the planning authority of the country. This therefore, imposes upon the financial institution due restraint as also exercise of prudence in the assessment of the schemes of deployment of finance by the intending borrowers. The financial institutions enjoy the blessings of the government and an assured flow of funds in the event of shortfall of internal finance of an institution caused by absence of the expected extent of repayment of funds by the borrowers by due dates or recycling of inter-institutional finance. The spurt of growth of economy of Japan is largely attributed to commercial banking in which institution enjoyed full support of the Japanese government to provide indirect finance to industries including term loans. But since the commercial banking in India was nurtured under the ideology of conservation and operated in the area of short-term and call financing, India had to reckon with the embedded limitations of the commercial banking sector and embarked on the policy of introducing development banking through the institution of non-bank financial intermediary, which brought about a regeneration of Indian economy, and this tended to usher in a new era of industrial finance in the economic profile of the country where entrepreneurial incentive received a new dynamism of exploring unchartered areas of promise and potentiality in the annals of economic development.

The dimension of contribution of the non-bank, development finance institution so far is quite impressive and it can well be discerned that development bank will be acclaimed as pillars of strength in the process of the reshaping the economy of the country.

MONETARY SYSTEM VIS-A-VIS INDIAN BANKING

In the monetary system of India the composition of

money market as well as capital market have undergone a sea-change in the post-independence period. The recognised sector of short-term money market comprise the term-deposit market, the inter-bank call money market, the treasury bills market, discount and re-discount institutions, and the central bank as the lender of last resort. Commercial banks are required to administer their resources within the regulatory framework of the governing laws, namely, the Reserve Bank of India Act and the Banking Regulation Act and the maintenance of rational level of liquidity is the catch-word of commercial banking. The authorities are obviously concerned to introduce innovations in the money market and in this effort the influence of the financial systems prevailing in the developed economies particularly, those of U.S.A., France, West Germany and Japan have a positive influence especially on the front of instruments and securitisation as apparatuses of operations of commercial banking. Stabilisation of money market is a *since qua non* of economic development and for this commercial banks need to be insulated against the cyclical disastrous jolts in the economy, more often than not, precipitated by the world economic order where pulls and pressures are ever active. Japan sets an example to protect the banking sector falling from their feet during the depression in 1970s resulting from the ruthless escalation of oil prices, by pumping money into the banking sector. Reserve Bank of India is generally prone to pursue a cautious policy of even operation of commercial banks and its powers of over-seeing were hardly relaxed, although the mechanism of control changed from time to time. The Credit Authorisation Scheme (CAS) is a glaring instance of credit control that caused not only hardship to the banking sector but entailed delayed lending and the borrower's woe was obvious. The Gadgil Committee almost a decade ago recommended for the abolition of CAS and willy-nilly CAS was abolished only in 1987 with a rejoinder that banks will be obliged to send statements of their lendings to such sector of borrowers hitherto coming within the operation of CAS and this smacks of *post-mortem* control effect. The recent raising of Cash Reserve Ratio (CRR) to 11% undoubtedly carries with it the ripples of conservation in banking and runs counter to the objective of liberalisation policy envisaged for the field of banking since its shackling effect cannot be over-looked. The massive investment to the tune of Rs. 649926 crores estimated for the Eighth Plan with an ambitious growth rate of 6% inevitably calls for a flexible, uninhibited money market and urges for the authorities to produce forward looking reforms in the financial system of the country having edifying effect befitting the dynamism of the national economic plan.

The Indian capital market, which has a positive upsurge is comprised of principally by development banking institutions, non-bank financial intermediaries, such as IDBI, IFCI, ICICI, IRBI, specific-term lending banks in the cooperative and agricultural sector and security houses. The profile resources of LIC, UTI, GCI term deposit with the government, have an enormous effect on capital market. The inter-corporate transfers are also a valued component of capital market. External sources of capital are signally important and India receives financial assistance from IBRD, IMF, IDA, Asian Development Bank, IFC, on multilateral basis and an enormous extent of financial aid committed by a large number of foreign countries by way of bilateral agreements. The government happens to be the largest supplier of capital in the public sector. The financial assistance stood at Rs. 5627 crores in 1986-87. In India, the position of unorganised capital market sector comprised of indigenous bankers and money lenders is of some significance particularly in the agricultural and small scale venture sectors. Experience shows that during the agriculture seasons the unorganised capital market sector is quite agog and active in order to reap a rich harvest out of financial assistance extended to the agrarian population who seem to be constrained to fall back upon the unorganised money lenders in order to meet the exigencies of its financial requirement, and in this game the loathsome, over-cautious, procedure bound dilatory and non-supportive attitude of the organised sector tends to keep the agriculturists at bay, since the large part of financial assistance of organised sector is in the form of refinancing term-loans and rediscounting of bills. Innovations in the form of instruments both in the money market and capital market are a notable feature about which an indicative picture has been given below. The capital market in India in all its appearance is fast forging ahead towards maturity and it can well be predicted that with due exercise of prudence and caution in the deployment of finance in the projects promising potential return and restructuring the existing projects to be viable by the amalgamation and merger of units and introducing largely the principles of "perestroika", the recent revolutionary thinking of U.S.S.R. capital market in India will have achieved a forceful acceleration to ensure a sound national economy in no-distant future.

EXTERNAL FINANCE

External finances are a very important component for any developing country. Two epoch-making international financial institutions setup at Bretton Woods more than 40 yeas ago, namely, the World Bank (IBRD) and the International Monetary Fund (IMF) with an unwaivering hope that these two institutions would drive away the usurious money lenders from "the temple of international finance," and assure the poor undeveloped countries to provide them finance to extricate themselves out of the rut of abominable poverty and deprivation. A massive financial assistance and aid was made to third world countries and India has been recipient of liberal financial assistance. One feature is however, notable that although the extent of utilisation of external assistance ranged from 40 per cent to 60 per cent of authorisation, nevertheless, India has not fallen from the grace of the two epoch-making world financing agencies. This position shows India's credibility in the world money market. Both the Institutions on the security of India's political and economic ideologies, have been satisfied that these are attuned to the objective for which the twins operate that is, alleviation of poverty and create a new India through pursuits of planned economy. The ideology of democratic socialism and diversified economic amelioration programmes being the watch word of free India are reckoned with as laudable and the philosophy has been accorded a general welcome and acceptability both by capital-minded industrialised countries and socialist countries which are now in the foreground. India, therefore, enjoys a comfortable position in the international area.

There have been kaleidoscopic changes in the scenario of international banking. Prior to World War II three were only two forms of international reserves, namely, gold and foreign exchange holdings of the monetary authorities where dominance of the US in respect of gold was patent, and the foreign exchange reserves were held by the leading currencies, namely, the US dollar and pound sterling of the U.S. But the world monetary agencies could no longer stick to gold reserve, and the declining stages of pound sterling provided a fillip to the US dollar to rule the roost, and the US dollar emerged as the dominating currency for the twin institutions. Reform in the international financing was an urgent need and this gave birth to the concept of the Special Drawing Rights (SDRS) conferring on the member-countries almost an automatic right to borrow funds from IMF in the event of their adverse balance of payments position. The developing countries do not have a good record of balance of payments position and this is due to many reasons principally, balance of trade deficit due to overdomestic consumption and non-preference for non-qualitative products of these countries in the international market, shrinking the scope for India's export expansion. This tends to bring about a volatile market position and fluctuating exchange rate. The developed countries are well aware of this disturbing position and SDRS operated in an expected condition and shibboleth of developing countries. The limitation of SDRS has, of late, been felt acute in as much as total allocation $ 21411 billion by two instalments in 1970-72 and in 1979-81 is considered too inadequate to hold the ground and there is a plausible case for enhancement of allocation for the purpose of SDRS. The conditionality attached to SDR is, horrowe, a recour for the recipiew countries while the prerogative of the creditor's surveillance over the debtor as to the deployment of funds borrowed under a given condition cannot be eschewed, nevertheless, some sort of self-denying ordinance on the part of the creditor can indeed, bring in an immense relief of tension of the debtor. A deregulated operational environment may not prove to be wholesome since the overdoing in an area will surely reflect it's ripple effect on another area and this tends to bring destabilising aspects of panic and uncertainty. The conditionality has to be softened to adapt to the realistic situation of borrowing countries. It is now advocated that the allocation of SDRS needs to be re-examined and increased to double the present quantum so that the needy poor and developing countries may get larger advances in future and thus chelee may be opportunity for international financial agency to give a stronger bite into the vital problem of alleviating the poverty of developing countries.

In spite of several international financing agencies, as affiliates and subsidiaries to the two parent institutions, such as, International Development Agency (IDA), International Finance Corporation (IFC), Asian Development Bank (ADB) and their relentless efforts to mobilise domestic and international resources and liberal outlook in approving the new investment projects, particularly by IFC during 1988-89, the industrialisation process in certain regions of the world e.g. in sub-saharan Africa, Latin American countries shows slothness.

Though South East Asia shows sign of a new outlook of aggressiveness towards industrialisation it is not very much evidently materialised except in Hong Kong, Taiwan and notably in South Korea, India has more or less an agreeable position and in spite of the high investment in capital intensive industries of controllable limits except in drought stricken periods contain volatility in the exchange rates and an appreciable balance of payments position after 1982-83 to enable it to build up exchange reserves to the tune of Rs. 6000 crores. The redeeming features, however, cannot overshadow India's mounting foreign debts and India stands out to be the largest debtor in Asia, and at present the extent of debt in Indian currency is Rs. 4500 crores and the debt is estimated to increase to 60 billion by the end of 1980-89 requiring a high debt servicing obligation.

This situation calls for monitoring the foreign loans by an aggressive surveillance over the deployment of foreign resources ensuring their profitable utilisation with hopeful generation of resources in economy for progressively easing out itself from the bulging burden of international debt which tends to eat out a part of fresh loans towards servicing the old debt.

PRESCRIPTIVE THINKING

Both IBRD and INF are presently plagued with the problems of reducing the debt burden of developing countries which has already swelled to 1.2 trillion. The matter has assumed such a proportion as to make it imperative for the world forces to propel themselves to find solutions to the debt problems of the developing countries, which are two-fold. On the one hand, existing debts are to be drastically reduced and on the other, effective strategy has got to be determined against relapse of the situation. But the matter is far from easy. In the recent (September 1988) East Berlin meet this issue received a pointed attention and gained a special emphasis. The minds of the participants however, were not *ad idem.* A group of 24 developing countries (G-24) led by Brazil Finance Minister, in which India took a leading part, expressed deep concern about the poverty debt-ridden third world countries which need supportive approach from the international financing authorities. Three strands of through emerged at the West Berlin meet, in which the most pertinent feature was the intention of internalisation of 'Ven' by Japan that attracted special attention of all participants. One of the thoughts that was given expression of the leading industralised countries to ease out the third world debts upto 500 million a year on a "case to case" basis and they did not subscribe to the view of blanket foregiveness. This education of debts, they argued can be achieved by multilateral cooperation. This was generally agreed upon by IBRD. The second thought emanated from the hard-hitting voice of a group of seven countries (G-7), namely, Britain, Canada, France, West Germany, Italy, Japan and the United State, which advocated for multicurrency operation instead of uni-domination, and urged for admission of Deusche mark of West Germany and Yen of Japan alongside the operating U.S. dollar. This group opined in favour of larger advances in future to the developing countries for their economic growth and not to leave them in the lurch. The debtor countries should be allowed to pay off their past debts gradually on voluntary basis and in some extreme cases the policy of "case to case" basis may be invoked. It was also urged that the middle income countries may be also allowed to enjoy debt forgiveness to a certain extent. The IMF did not rule out the possibility of such proposal. A third thought came partially from Japan and partially from India. Japan promised to lend its support to alleviate the poverty of the developing nations and one of the efforts will be to write off debts and interests incurred by the poorest nations between 1978 and 1987 which will be blanket forgiveness. 'Yen' will play a leading role in swinging funds to international money market and credit is likely to be made on a "case to case" basis to enable to recipient indebted countries to make structural adjustment programmes. IMF's Structural Adjustment Facility (SAF) stands in goods stead. Japan, a surplus country in Asia and one of the foremost developed economies of the world believes more in pragmatic approach to tackle an economic situation rather than dilate on theories, and to that direction 'Yen' is a cater. In the present situation, the IBRD takes more from the debtor counties than it gives to them. Those countries are in the cobweb of debts servicing and their structural adjustment programmes remain a far cry. India sounded a realistic note that official development assistance had stagnated in the range of 30 billion during the period 1980-86 and the situation needs immediate attention in order to flow funds to the developing countries, and suggested that as an incentive the World Bank should provide a special facility for the use of IDA reflows to subsidise interest rates on new debts and advocated for soft loans with confessional interest rates on future debts to the poor, developing countries.

IBRD and IMF though upto new control the international capital market as a result of multilateral combination and cooperation are, of late, by-passed by a large number of countries by way of their direct negotiation and bilateral financial agreements with the countries yearning for soft loans for specific projects as also general development process. This has, indeed not only complicated international accounting process but also has gone to devalue the world's biggest lending twins, though it may safely be predicted that these institutions control over the international market will remain unflattered for many more years to come although structural changes and adjustments attuned to world economic situation would be a concomitant necessity. The weakness of world economy pegged to single currency, that it is, US dollar became conspicuous in October 1987 when violent stock market swings due to speculative and arbitrage operations rocked that world market that threatened to precipitate recession in 1988-90. But happily that was averted by multilateral cooperation of the developed countries to save themselves from an awkward and obvious disaster. This event provided important lessons for the world financial market as to the necessity to safeguard it against volatility in exchange fluctuation by way of multi-currency control measures and also to realise that unregulated financial innovation being a significant contributor to the above event would be a potential danger to an even and balanced world money market. India, however remained unaffected by stock market swings of October, 1987. European Monetary System (EMS) a kingdom within a kingdom, conceived by EEC countries fortifies its constituent countries by their own process of mobilising funds and allocation thereof and ensure stable exchange rates by mutual understanding and EMS remained almost linscathed by the violent jolt of October, 1987 and the coordination policy of EMS are indeed, instructive in particular reference to widely fluctuating dollar and the narrowly fluctuating currencies of EMS.

It remains to be seen how the world institutions react to the various suggestions, advanced in West Berlin meet which intently cover two important aspects, namely, to reduce the debt-burden of the poor developing countries and enhancing the quantum of loans to these countries at lower rates of interest enabling them to restructure their economic schemes by liberalisation process, which of course, calls for abolition of inhibiting protectionism followed by developed countries by mutual agreement in order to protect the domestic markets of the European community and the U.S. and Canadian markets. Among the third world countries, India enjoys confidence of the world market and it can safely be predicted that flow of foreign funds is not likely to languish or wither away in a fareseeale future. India at this stage of aggressive industrialisation has necessarily to fall back on foreign funds for growth of infrastructure and critical and sophisticated technologically oriented industrial projects. IMF, of course, does not fight shy to stress the need of rigorous scrutiny and assessment of credibility of the borrowing countries and viability of their proposed projects before approving and allotment of IMF Fund. It can well be said that the currencies of Japan, Brazil and Korea, vying with each other to enter world market, would provide due acceleration and momentum of growth to the less industrialised countries, through the foreign industrial finance, and it may not be a small hope for the developing countries. Japan is likely to emerge as the locomotive force to drive ahead the Asian economy to the desired level of growth. ASEAN countries may also evolve to process for a common market mechanism to protect themselves from the swings of the world money market as such and in this direction Japan and India could obviously provide leadership.

NEW THOUGHTS ON INDIAN BANKING

Indian banking is reckoned with as vehicle of change as a catalyst of national economy. A vast volume of expectations have been attributed to the banking sector, some of which extend beyond the boundaries of banking proper. Many innovations have been conceived and introduced in Indian banking. Banks are to play the role of friend, philosopher and guide to investor, entrepreneur, household, and, small and neglected economic sector to make the Indian banking aggressive and dynamic. Innovative designs in Indian banking can be classified as: (i) institutional innovation through creation of specialised units for specific purposes, (ii) procedural innovations for quick, prompt and neat services, to customers, and (iii) innovations in instrument of banking operation for growth and control. Diversification is a pertinent aspect of Indian banking. Rural banking has stemmed from the concept of social banking and special emphasis has been laid on expansion of rural banking sector. Regional rural banks (RRBs) and NABARD have got to cater to the needs of agricultural sector as a matter of fulfilment of their objectives in as much as the agricultural credit of scheduled commercial banks ranged from 14 per cent to 20 per cent of gross bank credit during the past six years which is far from meeting the needs of this sector and his allows scope for indigenous bankers and village sahukars to take advantage of the situation in advancing various loans. The institution of regional rural banking is to have increased local involvement of banks for meeting the credit requirement of weaker sections and farming population. At the end of June, 1986, 194 such banks were working. They could mobilise deposits to the tune of Rs. 1286 crores and had outstanding advances to nearly Rs. 1408 crores indicating a credit-deposit ratio of 109 per cent. RRBs will have their positive stride to even out imbalances of distribution of bank credit, and hitherto neglected sectors will be highly benefited through the liberalisation policy in this direction. Indian banking as a whole will now be pressed into meeting the need of credit for village, will be served by some branch of bank and this scheme when implemented (likely to be in 1989) will undoubtedly be a Land mark in Indian banking to be more realistic. Merchant banking is a lofty innovation in Indian banking system. It is a specialised customer service scheme both as consultant and lender. In the expansion of banking business, securitisation by the process of under-writing of issue, leasing and housing financing constitute significant arms of activity. State Bank of India, as a biggest commercial bank in the country, set up a subsidiary, namely, SBI Capital Market Ltd. to play the role of merchant bank. The subsidiary unit was created as it was felt be SBI that merchant banking being a specialised customer service justice is possible if the job is taken out of the fold of the general commercial banking operation. The merchant banking has got its spurt in recent years and many leading commercial banks in the public sector and foreign banks operating in India have also started separate divisions for merchant banking. It can be expected that in times ahead, the operation of merchant banking will be assuming increasing importance in India banking system. Participation of Indian banks in under-writing of issues and in the policy of securitisation is fraught with danger in a highly speculative stock market operations, where the percentage of real transfer of scrips is very low being 4 per cent of the transaction on Bombay

Stock Exchange, 12 per cent on Calcutta Stock Exchange, and 14 per cent on Delhi, and this tends to be a strong factor of fluctuation of price and instability beyond expected range that may affect the values of holdings of the banks. A strong surveillance of RBI is called for in this area of operation of the banks. Most of the financial institutions participate in under-writing business and also hold shares in many corporate organisations as a measure of providing capital to them and also pumping funds in the capital market. Now, an institution, namely, Stock Holding Corporation of India (SHCI) has been set up to streamline the buying, selling and transfer of shares among the financial institutions such as, U.T.I., L.I.C., G.I.C., IDBI, IRBI and IFCI, through the operational relationship with stock brokers. The stock operations, thus, are to be brought within the operational functions of a central agency. Housing Promotion and Finance Corporation has been set up by SBI to operate in the field of housing finance. Some non-Indian Banks operating in India have also evidently gone for introducing many innovations in the banking sector, Grindlays. Standard Chartered and Hong Kong Ban are notable in this connection. Citibank and Canara Bank are also dynamic in this area. There is an obvious sympathic vibration and other banks are agog in introducing innovations of one kind or the other and the matter is catching on.

CHALLENGES TO INDIAN BANKING

Mobilisation of deposits, facility of quick credit and transferability of fund and rendering of customer service with a smile are the three parameters of successful banking. But the banks are confronted with constraints some of which are exogenous and beyond the control of bank management since directions and fiats for mandatory nature are flowing from the controlling authorities in the monetary system. At present, the household sector constitutes a very expanding source of funds and since many avenues have been opened unto this sector to choose the field of investment and deposit, the banking sector no longer enjoys the formidable position of depository. Apart from government instruments such as, National Saving Schemes, Vikas Patras, Rahat Patras, Kisan Patras which provide for tax incentive and other concessions, the impact of the recent liberalisation policy to allow the corporate sector including government companies to accept public deposits is keenly felt on the growth of bank deposits and the deposit growth rate has been registering a downward curve in as much as the rate has slowed down from 20 per cent in 1986 to 16 per cent in 1987. The term deposits in banking sector appear to have fallen the grace and choice of customers due to untempting interest rates compared to that in the other competing fields. The mere facility of withdrawal of term deposit at a discount before maturity is proving to be a poor incentive. UTI has been emerging as the strongest competitor in the money capital markets by throwing up many incentive schemes backed by fiscal incentives. UTI launched in association with Merrill Lynch in July 1986 the 'Indian Fund' providing facilities to NRIs and persons staying abroad to invent in securities markets in India. UTI also set up a 'Mutual Fund' in September, 1986 to provide a channel to small investors for investing in shares quoted in Stock Exchanges.UTI moblised Rs. 140 crores under the 'Indian Fund' and Rs. 150 crores under the 'Mutual Fund' UTI's operations are obviously a measure of short circuiting the operation of Indian banking as well as shedding direct financial responsibilities of the government in respect of capital and money markets.

Term-deposits are the obvious lendable bank resource towards expansion of credit including short term lending. (One of the aspects of liberalisation in the capital market lies in the invitation of Non-Resident Indian (NRIs) investable funds in India which is attended with liberalisation of fiscal policy. SBI issue of NRI bonds is significant. The banking in India is in syndrome in respect of interest rates, exchange rate fluctuations resulting from BOP position and viable banking *vis-a-vis* social banking touching the size of profitability interest rates have been conceived to be a variable depending upon the nature of deposits of credits. In case of NRI deposits the incentive of interest rate is attractive in as much as the interest rates were steadily reduced from 13 per cent to the present 9 per cent per annum. In other cases, in general, the highest rate of time deposits has been fixed at 10 per cent per annum. To charge differential lending interest rates in Indian banking is now an accepted policy, the minimum lending interest rate (MIR) has been fixed by RBI at 16 per cent. In order to implement the differential lending interest rates, grading of borrowers will be necessary corollary and it is propounded that borrowers are to be graded on the parameters of management accounting method of ratio analysis and the borrowers will be classified under categories "A plus", "A" "B Plus" "B" and "C" a number of Indian banks are inclined to scale the MIR and charge higher interest. The matter is not, however simplistic in view of competing operating banks in the field including the foreign banks operating in India. This freedom of banking sector out of apprehension of flight on siphoning off of customer's funds from one bank to another or from Indian banks to foreign banks in competitive banking situation. In fact, a section of foreign banks has welcomed this competitiveness in Indian banking. But the logic of differential lending interest rates is clear in a developing country in particular on the principle that the more able should bear the higher brunt of burden to sub-serve the interest of an egalitarian society, where the need of social banking happens to be an impelling necessity.

INSTRUMENTS

Indian financial system is more or less oriented to the multi-instrument operation. A number of instruments are already in vogue in the financial system. The Vaghul working group set up by RBI following the Chakraborty Committee Report, examined the aspects of development of instruments and recommended for activating the existing instruments and developing new instruments with a view to generating funds to the banking sector as also ensuring for it, enough flexibility as apart of liberalisation policy adopted in the case of banking in India. The Chakraborty Committee is in favour of banks freedom to determine interest rates and vary the rates according to fluctuations in 'business conditions and their own cost of funds'. The Vaghul Committee accordingly recommended for the revival of Participation Certificates (PCS) with a liberal approach to their operation delinking them largely from being counted as a part of time and demand liabilities and hence reserve requirements. PCs will inject liquidity and facilitate inter-bank lending. PCs being now in operation are an affair of RBI. They are not, however to be unregulated issues and their characteristics of maturity as Treasury Bills or call money will be well preserved. The new instruments which the Vaghul Committee has recommended for is the introduction of Commercial Paper (CP) which is reckoned with a liberalisation of banking policy as well as a step towards securitisation. Commercial Paper is to be introduced by he corporate sector as a short term money market, since this will be discountable instrument with characteristics of unsecured promissory notes with a fixed maturity not beyond three months. This will be a negotiable bearer instrument drawn upon a discounting bank. PCs are to be free from any trade transaction and can be issued by reliable corporate organisation in order to tide over temporary money constraint with full responsibility to redeem the issue. The recommendation for issue of PCs is, indeed, very lofty in Indian banking and it is based upon foreign experience where the issuer's financial soundness and veracity are less questionable. In advanced countries, however, PCs are but a concept with for less operational momentum. However, in the Indian situation, credit rating of the issuer will be an ardent necessity and the assistance of recognised credit rating agency as to the certification of the standing of the issuer will be needed to impart credibility to the CPs. The role of RBI's discount and Finance House of India (DFHI) will be very important in this area of operation of both PCs and CPs.

In this connection, it will be pertinent to note that despite the recommendation of the Tandon Committee and the Chore Committee for a ride of commercial bills, there has not been so far any buoyancy in the area of commercial bill financing. Now, with the increasing liberalisation policy in Indian banking and setting up special and specific 'funds' by UTI and the specialised DFHI it may be reasonably expected that commercial bill financing operating will receive necessary flurry in Indian banking. Credit cards industry is largely making its head way in Indian banking and it smacks of a GRID system to transferability of funds.

A plethora of instruments and securitisation aspects of financing are attended with problems of portfolio management in the banking sector, the twin problems are as to distribution of bank funds amongst the instruments and the extent of holdings of different types as instruments which can be wholesome to maintain liquidity and profitability of banking on an even keel, and this depends very much on the judgment of bank authorities to avert any possible crisis that may precipitate from the overshot of any particular instruments in bank finance in the event of short-run market fluctuations. The Credit Rating Information Service of India Limited (CRISIL) promoted by the joint efforts of the Indian Banks, non-bank financial inter-mechanical and foreign banking agencies can well be a positive guide to aid the Indian banks to keep the risks of market fluctuations of financial instruments at bay.

MECHANISATION

On the customer service front the mechanisation process has been gathering momentum. The Damle Committee, examined the feasibility of introducing suitable technology. Now, apart from introducing magnetic ink, standardisation process of cheques and bank documents, electronics and computerised operations are largely developing in the domain of banking. Though automation process is far, the teller system, inter-bank information technology expeditious currency swap facilitating covers for banks against exchange rate fluctuations, telephonic terminals *inter alia* are important facets of mechanisation in Indian banking. Expeditious operations being the catchword of successful banking today mechanisation must be reckoned as welcome device. Nevertheless, in a country like India, where the rate of unemployment is ever increasing huge employment opportunities have already been created to combat unemployment. There is need to strike out a balance between the launching of mechanical devices that go to replace manpower and shrink employment and absorption of manpower, and for this a careful study is called for in order to identify the banking operations as well as location where automation is more conducive towards meeting the customer needs.

But all said and done myriad innovations can little propel banking unless the driving force behind all this is bold, imaginative, and attitudinally congenial to.render satisfaction to different types and grades of bank customers who are looming large in a developing economy which factor urges for determining socially acceptable normative postulates in respect of modernisation and technology orientation in the banking sector.

The Report of Chakraborty Committee underlines the two important facets of Indian monetary system recoiling upon the Indian economy, namely, irrationality of money supply targeting and the interest rates being bogged down to the regulatory, subsidised approach to economy rather than allowing them to be amenable to market forces, and also acuteness of the inflation far exceeding tolerable limits averaging 9.8 per cent annum during the period 1970-71 and 1983-84 (at present it is 10% and there is already a warning from IBRD). The committee attributes the ills to unduly high rates of growth of money supply compared to the rate of growth of real output. The committee points out in discussing the scenario of the monetary system, the money price nexus and the resultant upward swing of he rate of inflation. While the real output from 1970-71 to 1982-83 grew at 3.7 per cent, the money supply at 17.2 per cent and inflation at 9.8 per cent per annum. The committee, while subscribing to the need of monetization of economy and injecting flexibility into the area of interest rates, it, however cautions the government against unregulated money supply and for that matter the government has to apply brakes on RBI borrowings and regulate import of funds from abroad by the plethora of institutions vying with each other to enter into the world money market.

Financial disciplines have to be strictly enforced in order to make the monetary system behave in compatibility with the dynamism of Indian economy. Pursuing a policy of self-reliance is a significant recommendation. It is, of course, easier said than done to separate chaff from the grain. National Finance Council set up by RBI following the Chakraborty Committee Report has examined the important issues relating to Term lending financial institutions *vis-a-vis* banking sector and liberalisation process that has already started in the banking sector aiming at how to take Indian banking out of the shackles of conservatism. The Chakraborty Committee was emphatic on demand function of money and tried to hold out the irrational monetary targeting may adversely recoil on the functioning of other economic sectors too. The Committee clarified that the phrase 'monetary targeting' is not to be equated with rigid target, and advocated for 'monetary targeting with feed back' in order to facilitate the smooth functioning of the other sectors of economy. The nexus of money supply prices, read with interest rates cannot be overlooked. But the important consideration is to determine 'whether causation runs from money to price or from price to money'. It argued that tests by economists so far in this regard are basically 'post-hoc, ergo propter hoc' variety and never conclusive. The reason is not far to seek in as much as in a situation of rapid transformation of national economy the variables tend to be too volatile to make it possible for one to project any conclusive test. Be that as it may, save exogenous factors, which have many crippling effects. The supply of M_3 can be controlled to a large extent been in a situation of pursuing a flexible regulation of money supply policy by virtue of control measures in the sensitive centres of economy such as public spending, non-plan expenditure, fiscal and the like, and, much wisdom is called for to make the economy resilient and striding without the teeth of establishing forces in the monetary system.

The Chakraborty Committee report recommends for banking institution in India to be profitable operation by exercising its freedom to charge varying lending interest rates depending on the status of borrowers. The report also favour competitiveness in banking to ensure efficiency in operation. The Committee is more in favour of timely and adequate supply of bank credit to the priority sector than allowing concessions in the interest rates on credit. Attributes of newness should, of course be reflected in bank operations. Chakraborty Committee appears to overlook social banking which cannot be jettisoned in a developing mixed economy, although that may go to crunch profitability of the banking sector and a paradoxical situation cannot be ruled out.

CONCLUSION

Indian banking may appear jejune in many respects. The notion of inter-bank competitiveness is largely erroneous in as much as the whole gamut of banking is under the control and surveillance of a central authority (RBI) where the banks are less free to move beyond the periphery of control structure and modalities. Banks as individual entities can, however, be pressed into competition to uplift their respective goodwill by demonstrating their efficiency in rendering quick rational and satisfying on the track service to their respective customers. Official policy thrust upon the banking sector some-times may weaken the banking sector. For example, the recent policy asking the banks to share with the financial institutions the woes of sick industrial units is undoubtedly an unwelcome direction to the banking sector. Moreover, it puts the cart before the horse in as much as restructure and streamlining of sick units on a ruthless consideration of potential viability should precede before the banks could be asked to irrigate this field. A sort of Russian 'Perestroika' is necessary with regard to sick units through schemes of amalgamation, merger change of management etc. The Board for Industrial and Financial Reconstruction (BIRF) is examining the issue. To ask banks to share the brunt of cost overruns of projects with the financial institutions is also incompatible with the basic objectives of commercial banks. Banking sector is visited with multiplicity in operational areas and goes in for a whole-hog doctrine, which is neither rational nor conductive to the objectives of banking. Liberalisation move should not be reckoned as conferring freedom the banking sector either to lay its hands on any financial deals or to overtop the limits of guiding policy. Restructuring the banking sector seems to be overdue. Maintaining individual entitles of public sector banks is a misnomer and it is time they be restructured. The concept of restructuring is studded with too many models and it is far from easy to conceive a rational model of restructuring the banking sector. Suriaya Commission and James Raj Committee recommended for restructuring the banking sector. Indian banks have to be restructured on a functional approach and regionalised sectoral banking activity. To allow a bank to open too many branches would be tainted with outflow of resources and making in road into finance of the bank without commensurate returns. Grading of banks on parameters of their standing and credit worthiness is necessary and functional areas are to be identified for each such grade so that overlapping activity of banks in a narrow geographical area may be staved off or minimised. Redistribution of banks on the basis of locational concept that is metropolis, urban, semi-urban and rural backward areas, may even out the present asymmetry lurking in respect of resources distribution, lending field and volume, interest rates generation priority lending considerations and viability of banking. Each grade of banks is to be placed under the umbrella of a christened apex authority in order to make the directive control of RBI effective through those few apex authorities relieving itself of the burden of controlling a large number of individual banks. Functional redistribution will also go to minimise the control centres. This suggestion of restructuring the banking sector resembles somewhat the present structure of GIC. Commercial bank individually hunting for foreign funds not only goes to destabilise external debt position and create inflationary spiral but also tends to weaken the bargaining position of soft loans from the international agencies through the aegis of the state.

Inflation is a game in the wider premises and spectrum of national economy, and banks can be hardly blamed in this respect when they are required to account for both new and recycled resources. Money supply target should be strictly adhered to and non-plan expenditure needs to be rationed in order to put restraint on excessive borrowing of the government and saddle itself with interest burden (net interest burden of Rs. 6900 crores will go to absorb 22 per cent of central tax receipts in 1988-89). The policy of liberalisation of import needs to be rationalised in order to improve B.O.P. position and the 'imported inflation' be averted by measure of augmentation to indigenous resource position. The role of Exim Bank in regard to accelerate export, particularly project export, reducing the appraisal time cannot be over emphasised. BOP position has got to be amply improved for the sake of fortifying the built-in foreign exchange reserves.

Inspite of numerous shortcomings prevailing now in the Indian banking, one can hardly overlook the spurt of development and acceleration of growth of India's national economy to which the contribution of the banking sector is of no mean order. Prolific enthusiasm and entrepreneurship generated by the Indian banks in society by demonstration of the changed attitude to operate as mass banking instead of hitherto class banking, although they are often times strait-jacked and left with Hobson's choice in the matter of operations by virtue of official policies, is undoubtedly be reckoned with a significant scenario in the domain of Indian banking today, which cannot be reproached for vexing fatigue as yet. And above all, the indiluted and firm faith reposed by society in Indian banks as depository and purveyor of finance epitomises the success of Indian banking and herein lies the splendour of the banking system of a developing economy that aims at moving toward a new millennium.

9

*Economic Commercialisation**

T.P. MAITIN**

I

INTRODUCTION

1. In keeping with the rich academic abilities of Dr. Rajbahak, combined with his high administrative skills, we purpose to share our views briefly on some important trends emerging in economy management of the country today and to offer an appropriate approach to meet effectively the challenge of development management.

2. The major theme of our lecture is commercialisation as a policy measure being increasingly adopted by larger group both under the public and private operational sectors of the economy. This trend has been of an unduly heavy reliance upon excessive exploitation

* The present paper is the full text of the lecture delivered by Prof. Maitin in the memory of Prof. R.P. Rajbahak.

** Professor of Commerce and Dean, Faculty of Commerce, Patna University, Patna.

of resources obviously much at the cost of the common population of the country.

3. What is the purpose of managing an economy? What do we expect from this system? Irrespective of the political ideologies governing the mechanism as well as the operations of this system, there must be certain fundamental aims, basic enough to fulfil the aspirations of a politically independent and economically self-reliant nation. Whether we succeed in our efforts to achieve these goals in a much different issues the immediate task should be at least to support and subscribe only those values which do not get an opportunity to work against the interests of a developing society as a negative force. It is in the same context that we also propose to analyse some of the common problems facing the challenge of academic management in the country.

II

INDO-NEPAL COOPERATION

1. India and Nepal are two different countries in the political sense. They, however, enjoy a common mythological base and uniform culture. They are also neighbours. But they are virtually one in terms of social, religious and economic values. For the people at large, they hardly find any difference between India and Nepal owing to the rich tradition of a bondage of mutual love and respect for each other.

2. Nepal is a land-locked country and it is the only Hindu Kingdom in the world. In view of its geographical limitations, however, it has necessarily to rely upon the assistance of others. Moreover, every development on the social, political or cultural front of its neighbours is an area of concen to Nepal. It has its own link which causes a chain of reactions in almost every sphere of opration. The interest of Nepal, therefore, is deeply involved in

almost every activity here and it continuously observes both the formulation and execution of our every policy. It is this which makes the task of diplomacy management as a serious challenge, particularly between India and Nepal.

3. Again, Nepal is a politically sensitive country. Like others, it has its own ego. Sometimes it may not demand; but it certainly expects. Relationship management with Nepal, therefore, is a highly delicate assignment. It needs a full understanding of the problems of Nepal on the one hand, and the possible channels of our fruitful cooperation to them on the other.

4. On many ocasions, even the senior diplomats may fail to appreciate the implications and intricacies of those issues which are realised by the common people of the two countries. This often gives birth to such confusions and contradictions on both the sides which could have been easily avoided through a more tactful handling of the situation. Besides trade relations, therefore, we have to continuously strengthen our social, therfore, we have to relations with Nepal. This just expects a better understanding of the issues affecting each other, mutual cooperation, political sympathy, joint goodwill, exchange of trust and confidence and frequent interaction of ideas.

III

RISK AND GAINS

1. Let us now address ourselves to a few problems of our own economy. A careful and honest self-assessment of the present economic system in the country immediately reveals some unpleasant risks here and there. While every effort towards a liberalised economic system with increasing emphasis on globalisation of trade and industry is logically commendable, the execution of announced policies and the resultant gains or losses too

have to be examined in a more independent manner. Sometimes, what may sound to be commendable in principle may not be actually so in practice. After all, there are some established norms of evaluation of economic progress which have to justify our monetary and fiscal policies. The principles of financial management of a country are almost universal in their application.

2. Inflation and rising prices, which are detrimental to the very suvival of mankind on the domestic front, never accept an economic policy which may have an international outlook based on the guidelines issued by foreign agencies. Internal economic satisfaction perhaps is the first and foremost task of planning; it is only after our own needs and aspirations have been met reasonably well that we can enter into the strategies of international marketing.

3. India today has some of the best brains in the world, if not any thing else. The actual contents, however, may not be known to the people outside this circle. Then how do we display our intellectual capacity and moral maturity to the people who somehow still believe that the country can not prosper without foreign assistance? If huge flow of funds to the capital market and sizeable over-subscriptions to corporate issues of any indicator of industrial prosperity, India is no longer an economically poor country, either in tems of financial resources, technical skill or professional expertise. Even the best of the agencies operating in the capital market today have not yet been able to mobilise fully these financial, technical and professional resources available at our command. Let us, therefore, underline this thought very firmly that India has to develop through its own talents and in no area they should be treated as inferior to the supply of any other goods or services floating in the open market.

4. Undoubtedly, profitability is the best form of motivation to entrepreneurship. This is the only incentive which offers adequate initiative and encourages people to

come forward towards a productive participation in the programmes of development. It is perhaps this theory which often misguides the policy of excessive commercialisation. It is one thing to minimise the cost of production, charge maximum prices from the consumers, generate larger profits for the organisation, disburse higher amount of pay and allowances to staff, create substantial amount of reserves and distribute handsome dividend to the shareholders.

5. To continue the same process further, it is just one thing to enjoy the rising prices of its equity in the stock exchange; but much different when the company itself decides to sell its securities at substantially higher rates of premium through public issues, leaving a very little margin for the prospective shareholders of the capital market as an incentive to save and invest and to participate in the risks involved in the stock trading business. For a very long time in the history of investments, shareholders have combined their fortunes with the fluctuating trends of security prices in the stock exchange. The losses or gains in such movements have been solely covered by the securityholders. With the current system being continuously adopted by a larger number of companies which are now offering their shares at maximum possible premium, the tendency is obviously towards centralisation of economic powers with the concurrence of concerned authorities.

6. While a substantial portion of the current appreciation in the market price of securities is being consumed by the companies themselves, very little is being left for the prospective investors. Moreover, with the type of securities scam in the background involving the highest possible level of corruption and misappropriation in the economic management system, there is absolutely no guarantee that prices of such issues will not decline in the future and thereby cause substantial loss to the investor without in any way affecting the corporate giants who have alrady

accumulated the huge premium surplus collected from the market. Even the decline in equity pricesmay be a manipulated and calculated stake through artificial twists in the stock exchange operations to consolidate futher gains.

7. Thus, if the capital market is still accepted as a substantial indicator of economic progress in the country, India has made distinctive achievements in this direction. A tremendous amount of responsiveness to security issues may be easily witnessed today. Increasing participation of people in the programmes of corporate financing is an unprecedented involvement. This has created a new awareness towards savings and investment in the society and all efforts need to be channelised to consolidate this awareness in the future as well.

8. This, however, has also brought into focus the importance of proper management of corporate enterprises so that the investors and the shareholders are able to receive adequate returns from their outlay. Those who come out with their funds and extent them to the corporate sector not only expect a sizable dividend, but also carry a common objective of earliest capital appreciation. Instead of being genuine investors closely interested in the long-term operational activities of the company, their interest often remains confined to an immediate increase in the security prices which they intend to unload as quickly as possible. Moreover, participation in the management efficiency of a company producing substantial profits is a democratic right of the shareholders and it should not be confined to benefit only a few.

IV

PARALLEL ADMINISTRATION

1. Of late, a new form of development is being identified in the country. To some, it may appear to be a trend towards

privatisation. But it also means a policy of excessive commercialisation in administration. Quite a good number of essential activities which for a very long period in the economic history of the country were considered to be exclusive areas of state responsibility are bing gradually managed by a fast emerging parallel system.

2. This form of administrative substitution encouraged by the Government has raised many pertinent questions. Are we shifting some of our fundamental duties to the private operators for obtaining additional efficiency and supplementary support? Does the state intend to share the prosperity of the private sector which is obviously coming out of a well-organised exploitation of the masses? Are we evolving a system of economic collaboration where the primary responsibility of the state will be discharged by the private agencies and the state will only participate in the surplus profit generated by the policy of excessive commercialisation obviously endorsed and silently supported by the Government? Does it represent a voluntary failure of the state machinery in providing a capable or effective management of basic affairs?

3. Let us now substantiate our arguments. The following table shows some of the essential activities traditionally assigned to state administration and their latest substitutes being gradually established as an alternative system of the economy.

Alternative Management

Service	*Substitute*
1. Police	Private Security Agencies
2. Post and Telegraph	Private Couriers
3. Railways	Transport Service
4. Diplomatic Missions	Lobbying Contractors
5. Electricity	Common Generators
6. Water Supply	Private Boring and Storage
7. Television	Dish Antenna and Cable Channels
8. Airlines	Private Flight Operators
9. Hospitals	Nursing Homes
10. Schools and Colleges	Coaching Institutes

4. There are many other examples which may be included in this table. It would appear that sometimes the alternative systems have assumed a more significant and prominent role in the economy than the original itself. This simply indicates that we are now fast moving towards a country in search of alternatives. This deserves a serious thinking on our part. To what extent a country should allow or tolerate a parallel administrative structure of this nature? Is it a system which enjoys complete freedom to exploit the consumers. It would be still more interesting to observe here that privatisation and commercialisation of this nature has offered immense opportunities to enhance the service charges of the Government operations as well in conformity with the charges realised by the private agencies. Perhaps both now join together drawing inspiration from each other to raise the cost of their services to the optimum possible extent.

5. Unfortunately, this is a reserve trend. The pricing policy of essential services should have been guided and governed by the Government granting due protection to the people at large. In the existing system, however, the private operators control the pricing pattern of basic services, and the state faithfully follows it. The outcome is quite natural—a continuously rising trend of cost of services in the economy as a price of growth. Even in terms of the standards of performance, the state departments often ignore any efficiency of quality consciousness in programmes and production.

6. From the point of view of reliability, efficiency, economy or subsequent accountability, it is invariably the alternative which is more dependable. Excessive commercialisation, therefore, appears to be the most common goal of both the Government and the private sector. This ultimately makes people suffer. Moreover, such collaborations seldom allow any healthy competition among the operators to any possible benefit of the consumers. This is yet another area of challenge to the

policy of commercialisation which is being thrown into the operational economy and which deserves serious attention.

V

CONCLUSION

In order to sum-up our entire discussion on the growing tendency of excessive commercialisation in the economy, we may now draw the following conclusions:

(i) Cooperation between India and Nepal is an essential aspect of economy management; it needs social, religious and cultural approach rather than crude bureaucracy or o

(ii) Development of capital market and enormous participation of people in investment programmes should not be allowed to be misused as a channel of concentrated gains.

(iii) Management of essential activities need to be more cost-effective; shifting of such responsibilities to the private operators does not serve the purpose in a realistic manner.

The immediate approach, therefore, should be how to check effectively the growing emphasis on commercialisation policy (much to the disadvantage of the economy in general) for the purpose of achieving a more balanced distribution of resources as well as opportunities at every level of society. The dynamics of development today is governed more by moderation of attitudes and protection of ethical values to attain stability rather than by mere multiplicity of policies pronouncements.

Ladies and gentlemen! this brings us to the close of our present analysis incorporating some of our views of the current state of the economy. Our purpose has been to identify issues, indicate the gaps, initiate a more fruitful dialogue and invite you—the experts—to join hands in suggesting the best possible lines of action. Yet, sound management of a developing economy like that of India is a continuous process; it is also a common challenge to all those who either support or oppose a political ideology. Thus, participation in administration may be either direct or indirect, the effective and efficient management of the entire economic system must be a consolidated activity, a cooperative affair and a comprehensive commitment to the society in general.

I once again pay my homage to late Dr. Rajbahak in whose memory I have been able to talk to you on the present theme. I also have my most sincere thanks to the organisers of this conference who have given me an opportunity to deliver this lecture. Thank you very much ladies and gentlemen.

Index